Exercising Agency

Exercising Agency

Decision Making and Project Initiation

MARK MULLALY

Routledge
Taylor & Francis Group

LONDON AND NEW YORK

First published in paperback 2024

First published 2015 by Gower Publishing

Published 2016 by Routledge
4 Park Square, Milton Park, Abingdon, Oxon OX14 4RN

and by Routledge
605 Third Avenue, New York, NY 10158

Routledge is an imprint of the Taylor & Francis Group, an informa business

Publisher's Note
The publisher has gone to great lengths to ensure the quality of this reprint but points out that some imperfections in the original copies may be apparent.

British Library Cataloguing in Publication Data
A catalogue record for this book is available from the British Library.

Library of Congress Cataloging-in-Publication Data
Mullaly, Mark.
Exercising agency : decision making and project initiation / by Mark Mullaly.
    pages cm
    Includes bibliographical references and index.
    ISBN 978-1-4724-2788-5 (hardback : alk. paper) – ISBN 978-1-4724-2790-8 (ebook) – ISBN 978-1-4724-2789-2 (epub)
  1. Project management – Decision making. 2. Decision making. I. Title.

    HD69.P75M854 2015
    658.4'03–dc23

                                                                    2014029455

ISBN: 978-1-4724-2788-5 (hbk)
ISBN: 978-1-03-283711-6 (pbk)
ISBN: 978-1-315-58141-5 (ebk)

DOI: 10.4324/9781315581415

Contents

List of Figures

List of Tables

Acknowledgements

With sincere thanks to the women in my life, without whom this book would not exist.

To Helen Morley, friend and collaborator, who provided invaluable support in enabling me to use Insights Discovery.

To Inez Brady, friend, colleague and statistician *par excellence*, for helping to make sense of what I was seeing, and helping to make the story that emerged as compelling and meaningful as what is contained here.

To Janice Thomas, an enthusiastic research partner for many years, a remarkably tolerant and patient thesis adviser, an unwavering champion of my abilities, an extraordinary mentor, and above all, a very dear friend.

And most particularly, to Dianne Ingram. You have supported me from the outset, believed in me, encouraged me, loved me and shared your life with me. For that I owe the greatest thanks of all.

Reviews of *Exercising Agency*

Strategy happens via projects. How strategy drives project initiation is a missing link in understanding between strategy-formulation and project-management. This study uses real-life experiences to theorise this process. Organisations and processes are important, but much is about individuals, their personality and their sense of agency. A very useful book for both academics and students who want to understand project initiation in practice, and practitioners who want to understand rigorously how to make decisions better.

Terry Williams, Hull University Business School, UK

Want to have a serious impact on your business? This book gives you a path to becoming an 'agent for the right change'; leading decision makers to identify projects that are worth doing and are likely to be successful. What a rare skill that is – incredibly important for you and the people you work for.

Dave Garrett, CEO, ProjectManagement.com

Exercising Agency *should be a required text in MBA schools and advanced project management training the world over. With a large proportion of all organizational work taking place in projects, we do a woefully inadequate job of preparing executives to select and initiate valuable projects. A work of unique breadth and depth, this book delivers a cogent review of relevant project and strategy literature supported by detailed original research that provides solid practical advice to those charged with making difficult project initiation decisions.*

Janice Thomas, Athabasca University, Canada

This book should be on the must-read list of every academic and reflective practitioner engaged in project organising work. Its emphasis is on how agency and rules influence decision making, at the project initiation stage, significantly shaping project delivery success or failure.

It provides a much needed reference and in-depth treatment of how decisions about the purpose of projects are crafted. It provides new empirical evidence that is convincing based on Mark's PhD thesis. I have already directed my PhD students interested in this topic to read the book.

Derek H.T. Walker, RMIT University, Australia

While many commentators have stressed the importance of the formation phase to project success, nobody has delved so enthusiastically into the complex interactions of politics and rules, and the agency of the individual project shaper, in the way Mark Mullaly does in this fascinating study of the decision-making world of project start-up.

Charles Smith, independent researcher and author

Chapter 1

Introduction

Understanding Initiation

This is a book about decision making. In particular, it looks in detail at how a very important type of organizational decision gets made: whether or not to initiate a project. Projects are about how strategy is implemented. Projects are the means by which change is initiated. Projects are about how new capabilities get created. Understanding how projects are initiated is therefore extremely useful. Interestingly, it is not something that has been comprehensively explored. Project initiation decisions live in a middle space between strategy development on one hand and project management on the other. They represent the critical transition point of when strategy begins to gain traction, and projects that respond to strategy begin to move forward.

This is also a book about how politics, process and personal influence combine to influence the conduct of project initiation. These influences are not always obvious, and they do not necessarily work in the way that many of us might predict. While many organizations profess to employ robust processes and rational analysis, the reality is that a significant number do not. Politics can play a strong role in influencing project initiation outcomes, and at the same time politics can also derail effective decision making. Individual actors in organizations also play a role. Depending upon the actor, that role might augment other influences, it might confound them, and in some instances it is the only way in which things actually get done.

The up-front process of initiation has been identified as having a dominant influence in determining the success or failure of individual project efforts. This book focuses on the process of project initiation: it seeks to explore the rule systems that influence how projects are initiated, the roles that are involved in project initiation, and how individual actors perceive and approach their roles. The book offers a substantive theory of how agency and rule emphasis influence the effectiveness of project initiation decisions. Based upon these insights, it offers practical guidance for those who are involved in shaping projects, the executives who approve them and the organizations that endeavour to improve how initiation decisions are made.

The Need to Make Initiation Decisions

An important theme that has emerged in connecting the initiation of specific projects with the larger purpose of the organization is the assertion that projects are a vehicle for delivering organizational strategy. This is often phrased as the need to ensure that the right projects are being done in the right way (Artto & Wikström, 2005; Aubry et al., 2012; Cooper et al., 2000; Crawford et al., 2006a). In part, linking projects with strategy responds to a recognition that for projects to proceed, they should in some way be responsive to the objectives and goals of the organization. If we accept that projects are being undertaken for a purpose, then the linkage between the project and the organization's strategy needs to be more broadly understood (Morris et al., 2006). This notion is also supported by the fact that the study of project failure shows that the causes of failure are more often strategic rather than technical, and are therefore likely the product of political processes within the organization (Cicmil & Hodgson, 2006). Linking projects with strategy not only connects projects with a sense of organizational purpose, but also firmly grounds project initiation within the political environment of the organization.

There is a fundamental question, however, of how this is done. There are many arguments about how the strategic alignment of projects *should* work. There are suggestions that project and organizational strategy need and should have two-way alignment processes that integrate views of policy, strategy and capability development (Maylor, 2001; Milosevic & Srivannaboon, 2006). Other studies go so far as to explicitly claim that projects are a means of implementing organizational strategy, even while recognizing that project management itself is not viewed from a strategic perspective (Aubry et al., 2012); this reinforces observations by Thomas et al. (2002) on the challenges of selling project management as a strategic capability to senior executives. When projects and project management do attain organizational focus, it tends to be more in response to crises than naturally perceived alignments; senior executives often fail to see the connection between project management and the goals of the organization (Thomas et al., 2002). The risk is that while projects are philosophically presented as proactive means of delivering strategy, they are more often practically seen as means of reacting to tactical and operational crises.

One means of attempting to reconcile these perspectives has been through the exploration of project governance. The concept of project governance largely addresses the oversight of projects, rather than being involved with the actual delivery. The role of governance in a project context includes choosing the right projects and establishing the correct objectives in response to organizational priorities and strategies; ensuring the appropriate allocation of resources; establishing appropriate strategies for reporting, and ensuring the projects and their results are sustainable (Morris et al., 2006; Williams et al., 2010). While these processes are again often expressed as being rational and normative in nature, there is also a strong political dimension that needs to be understood and investigated further (Flyvbjerg et al., 2003). As an example, one study found within one of its case studies that even where rational decision making was applied, the final decision was always a political one (Williams et al., 2010). This again reinforces the need to understand the political forces by which projects are initiated.

Exploration of the political and power dynamics that underlie purported rational approaches to governance include in particular their use as a source for legitimization of the project, or as a tool for reassurance of project owners (Williams et al., 2010). This notion is reinforced by observations that legitimization can be seen as a key focus for project management as a whole (Cicmil et al., 2009; Thomas, 1998), providing a façade for rationalism, power, efficiency and control. One of the rationales for project governance is that it serves to ensure that projects do not fail; it must 'prevent their birth, weeding out those projects that do not adequately address strategic aims, and destroying the seeds of failure before they can germinate' (Smith & Winter, 2010, p. 48). This is achieved through the introduction of stage-gating or gatekeeping mentalities. In many instances, however, these frameworks are seen more as boundary systems between executives and staff that enable executives to stay distant from the actual work of implementation (Artto et al., 2011). The danger, then, is that rational approaches are used to legitimize or justify project decisions without addressing the underlying complexities and political influences that are actually present, and idealized views of what should happen supplant an understanding of what actually occurs.

What We Already Know about Decision Making

While many in the field of project management have identified the need to better understand decision making within projects, and particularly how initiation decisions are made, there is a lot that we already know and understand about decision making. Decision making and project management actually share a common history, with both practices evolving out of the field of operations research in the years following the Second World War (Simon, 1965; Simon, 1987). Despite this common history, these fields have remained largely separate and distinct, with little overlap of research interest or subject matter content. Decision making has none the less developed into a rich field with much to offer in terms of insight and perspective on project initiation decisions.

Decision making in an economic and strategic context goes back more than 250 years, to a paper by Bernoulli to the 1738 proceedings of the Royal Academy of Science in St Petersburg. In a corporate and managerial context, the initial principles of decision making can be found in the work of Fayol (1949), who defined managerial activities as including planning, organization, command, co-ordination and control. The first direct definition of decision making, however, is found in the works of Barnard, who identified the role of decision making as one of the chief functions of the executive (Barnard, 1938), and made explicit the idea of decision as the delineation of ends – the objective to be realized – and means – the methods to be employed – that is the essence of much subsequent exploration of decision making. In particular, Barnard distinguished between the principles of decision making by the individual and those made on behalf of, or in the interests of, the organization. In a discussion of the decision making environment, Barnard states: 'within organizations, especially of complex types, there is a technique of decision, an organizational process of thinking, which may not be analogous to that of the individual' (139).

The principles of rational decision making in an economic context have their foundation in the work of von Neumann and Morgenstern (1944), who first advanced the notion of economic utility as a means of objectively measuring and quantifying the value of personal preferences. Fundamental to the models of rational decision making and choice is the idea of 'economic man' who, in being economic, is also 'rational'. Faced with an array of different, specified options, each option of which has different consequences attached to it, 'economic man' has a system of preferences against which the consequences of each option are evaluated, from which the option with the highest expected value is selected (Cyert et al., 1956; Simon, 1955). Rational decision making has faced extensive criticism (admittedly, largely from advocates for other models of decision making, and particularly behaviouralist models). Chief among these criticisms is the contention that rational models of decision making do not reflect how decisions are actually made (Simon, 1955; Simon, 1959). In particular, advocates of behavioural decision making argue that rational approaches ignore the fact that decision makers possess modest calculation powers, and that a normative theory – if it is to be useful – should only call for information that can reasonably be obtained and calculations that can actually be performed (Simon, 1965). In fact, research showed attempts at rationality lead to less effective decisions; empirical studies found that the comprehensiveness of analysis called for in rational models had a consistently negative relationship with performance (Fredrickson, 1984; Fredrickson & Mitchell, 1984). The implication is that decision making is complex, difficult, subjective and inconsistent, and that accurate understanding of decision making requires explicitly embracing the psychological complexity and strategies for simplification that underlie how decisions are actually made by individual actors in real world situations.

Behavioural decision making models emerged as a reaction to the rational models that had previously dominated perspectives of decision making. A fundamental consideration in the development of behavioural models was that they were based upon the capacity and limitations of human perception, and that perceived reality was vastly different from the 'real' world (Simon, 1959; Simon, 1965). Unlike the idealistic presumptions of perfect data and comprehensive analysis associated with rational techniques, behavioural decision making approaches are rooted in the limitations and constraints faced by actors constrained by limited cognitive capacity. One of the early explorations of behavioural decision making principles was the landmark book *Administrative Behavior* by Herbert A. Simon (Simon, 1947/1997), who argued that the limits of knowledge regarding means and consequences meant that rationality was at best approximate. This laid the foundation for the later work of March & Simon (1993), who fully developed the concept of 'bounded rationality'. Key concepts that are identified in bounded rationality are 'satisficing' – where decision makers accept a 'good enough' decision rather than seeking the best decision – and 'sequential search' – which recognizes that decision makers view available options one at a time, rather than comprehensively reviewing all options. Bounded rationality acknowledges that decision making is based upon incomplete information about alternatives and their consequences, and that information is not innocent: it is the product of different coalitions in organizations pursuing differing objectives (March, 1987). Unlike the idealistic presumptions of perfect data and comprehensive analysis associated with rational techniques, behavioural decision making approaches are rooted in the limitations faced by actors constrained by limited cognitive capacity.

While bounded rationality is designed to address the physical and practical limitations associated with decision making, the development of understanding of cognitive biases, heuristics and frames has been another significant area of development within behavioural theories of decision making. Historically, most of the literature dealing with risky choice assumed a decision maker who was risk-averse, an assumption that once again did not align with observed behaviour. This led to the development of cognitive decision models, which were particularly developed through the work of Kahneman & Tversky (1979) and their ground-breaking framing of 'prospect theory'. Prospect theory endeavours to provide a cognitively realistic view of how individual actors approach decision making when faced with possible gains and losses, and the fact that each of these appear to result in preferences for different strategies. Prospect theory consciously breaks the decision making process into two distinct stages: editing and evaluation. Editing is the process of choosing what inputs into the decision making process will be used, while evaluation reflects the actual selection based upon the edited prospects. Prospect theory also involves processes of simplification, where preferences and outcomes are rounded rather than retaining their initial precision, and where extremely unlikely prospects tend to be eliminated. It explicitly allows for the theory of bounded rationality, recognizing the inherent challenges of making risk-based or ambiguous judgements (Kahneman, 2003) while embracing many of the principles of cognitive bias that have been observed, but otherwise not explained. The implication is that cognitive decision models in general, and prospect theory in particular, provide a complementary perspective to other views of behavioural decision making.

Many of the behavioural decision making theories that have been developed thus far reflect a decision maker trying to make the best decisions possible (in other words, to maximize the results of the decision making process) in the face of limitations of information, knowledge, cognition and calculative capacity. A number of alternative decision making models have also emerged which consciously rejected the underlying assumptions of both rational and behavioural decision making, and which can perhaps best, or at least generously, be described as 'anarchic'. The best-known of these is the 'garbage can model' (Cohen et al., 1972), which was influenced in part by the experiences of March following his assumption of the position of dean of a university business school. The major feature of the garbage can model is the uncoupling of problems and choices, and throwing whatever else happens to be around at the time into a can to see what sticks to what. The garbage can model radically expanded on the assertion of Cyert and March (1992) that organizations do not have fully consistent goals; it developed the notion of 'loose coupling' among problems, participants, solutions and decisions (Gavetti et al., 2007). A temporal theory of decision making, the garbage can model deliberately rejected the ends–means model that had guided much of decision making.

The mix of garbage in a single can depends on the mix of cans available, on the labels attached to the alternative cans, on what garbage is currently being produced, and on the speed with which garbage is collected and removed from the scene. (Cohen et al., 1972, p. 2)

Problems were 'resolved' when any particular combination of problem, solution and decision maker interacted with each other in a decision making environment where there was a sufficient level of effort to get something done.

The garbage can model was viewed by some as going too far in its rejection of the essential features of decision making behaviour. While critics recognized that organizations do create problems, successes, threats and opportunities as a justification for their actions, they felt that there was a need to retreat from the full anarchy proposed by the garbage can model: 'This backtracking occurs because the garbage can model understates cause-effect attributions, de-emphasizes the activities preceding decisions, and ignores the activities following decisions' (Starbuck, 1983, p. 91). The anarchic models feel unfamiliar to some, in that they deliberately break the construct of means–ends that has been the hallmark of traditional perspectives since the earliest rational decision making models; what they do provide, however, is other insights into the dynamics of decision making encountered within the structural realities and limitations of organizations. Most importantly, they provide alternative perspectives for how decision making processes may be perceived, and how actors may view the dynamics underlying the making of decisions.

Considering the decision process associated with project initiation, none of the models discussed above fully offers a relevant framework. The process of initiation for any complex project clearly cannot be considered to be rational; too much is unknown and uncertain about both options and consequences. While the behavioural models consciously reflect the cognitive and capacity limitations inherent in project initiation choices, they do not provide contextual guidance as to how a decision maker would prefer one project over another. The anarchic model, while perhaps appealing in its description of decision making as a random intersection of problems, choices, decision makers and opportunities, removes the means–end focus that is still in part a consideration of evaluating projects. A sensible compromise within the literature as articulated would appear to be in part offered through an understanding of the principles of rule following originally articulated by Cyert & March (1992); rule following would appear to offer a middle ground between a purely means–end-based presumption of how individual decisions are made and a broader contextual understanding of the forces that influence decision making in organizational contexts.

The discussion of organizational routines, or decision making as rule following, presents a modification to behavioural decision making models. This concept first emerged in *A Behavioral Theory of the Firm* by Cyert & March (1992). The central principle of rule-following behaviour is that, in addition to the universally bounded nature of rationality, 'behaviours get programmed through spontaneous habits, professional norms, education, training, precedents, traditions, and rituals as well as through formalized procedures' (Starbuck, 1983, p. 93). Rule following in decision making emerged from the introduction of the principles of evolutionary theory to sociology. The essential premise was that a firm operates according to a set of decision rules that link a range of environmental stimuli to a range of responses on the part of firms (Nelson & Winter, 1974). The assumption that firms have decision rules, and that these are in turn retained or replaced through satisficing, provides a basis for both stability and ongoing evolution (Winter, 1971). Rule following therefore respects and reinforces the traditions of behavioural models, while providing a larger contextual appreciation of the influences of the organization on how decisions are ultimately made.

The development and use of rules in decision making draws from principles of bounded rationality. Decision making can be costly, and reliance upon simple rules to guide decision making is a form of cost minimization; it results in economies in terms of information collection, computation and communication, and provides frameworks in which actors throughout the organization are able to perform their roles with greater confidence and certainty (Winter, 1971). Burns & Dietz (1992) defined sets of rules as representing 'institutions': these entities collectively defined the settings or context of interaction, the actors who might take part and the rules for behaviour of roles within that context or setting. An important consideration in the understanding of rules and rule following is their application to the concept of 'agency'. Agency tends to assume that social actors have limited room for decision making, autonomy or creativity; actors are 'programmed' by the culture, and their ability to operate is limited by these constraints (Burns & Dietz, 1992). If this were true, behaviours would be entirely predictable with sufficient information; at the same time, it would be equally unsatisfactory to assume that agency was completely unpredictable and unlimited.

However strongly actions are patterned by rules, social life is sufficiently complex that some interpretation is required in applying rules to a specific action and interaction context. This inter-operation allows some variability in action from individual to individual, and a limited role for agency (Burns & Dietz, 1992, p. 273).

Dietz & Burns (1992) suggest that there are four criteria to be met in order to attribute agency to a social actor: the actor must be able to make a difference; the actions must be intentional; there must be room for free play on the part of the actor, and the actor must be reflexive. This expands the understanding of rule following to allow for variation in how an individual actor will interpret his or her context, select the appropriate rules and ultimately choose to act. It also implies that rules operate and are operationalized on multiple levels: there is an ideal in the context of the organization, interpretation of that ideal on the part of individual actors, and the actual behaviours that are encountered in decision making scenarios.

The development of rules and the adoption of routinized behaviours can emerge in response to a number of different mechanisms, including, in particular: active search for appropriate rules to co-ordinate collective action; passive adaptation to orders and rules issued by an external authority, and internal adoption through imitation, often with a low level of comprehension and conscious awareness (Cohen et al., 1996). The processes by which rules are generated, selected and transmitted influence the cultural environment of the organization; selection processes favour some rules, which leads to their increased prevalence, reflecting reproductive success or cultural fitness (Burns & Dietz, 1992). Burns & Dietz (1992) argue that no situation is totally unambiguous, and therefore there are multiple roles – and multiple rules – that can be operative, and which will thus govern behaviour. This process is not mechanical, but involves interpretation of context and role, and determination of appropriate action. Acting on rules is a particularly important force, and one related to power; actions that implement rules in turn produce responses from other actors and the overall environment, which may in turn cause an actor to modify or discard some rule or set of rules. The evolution or extinction of rules is therefore a product of understanding what works, and particularly an appreciation of what works in a particular context.

In exploring how initiation decisions get made, it is important to take into consideration the extensive insights that have already been developed about how decision making is actually accomplished in real-world situations, particularly in organizations. Decision makers are not able to fully evaluate every alternative; they lack the information, the computational capacity and the inclination to do so. While decision making is rationally bounded, it is also structurally influenced; conflicting goals in organizations mean that problems, solutions, actors and decision makers all compete for attention and focus. Rules and decision routines provide a means of providing this focus, helping decision makers to evaluate situation and context, assess their own roles and influence, and the options available to them based upon the interpretations available. Understanding how project initiation decisions get made must therefore take into consideration the structure and context of organizations, the process and rule environments that exist within those organizations, and the power and influence of individual actors in assessing their options and choosing their actions.

The Importance of Understanding How Initiation Decisions are Made

The research on which this book is based began with a desire to better understand decision making, and particularly the means through which project initiation decisions evolve. While there is a clear call within the project management literature to further explore the project initiation process, to date few studies have actually focused upon understanding the dynamics of this process and its underlying influences. Drawing on the literature of project management and decision making, this research study was framed to examine the influences of organizational rule systems and personal influences on project initiation decisions.

UNDERSTANDING THE INFLUENCE OF POWER AND POLITICS ON PROJECT INITIATION

Within the project management literature, there have been several calls to explore and better understand the influence of power dynamics (Cicmil & Hodgson, 2006; Walker et al., 2008a; Walker et al., 2008b). It has been suggested that power and politics have a significant influence on the governance and management of projects, and provide support for on-going legitimization of projects and practices (Cicmil et al., 2009; Thomas, 1998; Williams et al., 2010). The decision making literature also provides support for the notion of legitimization as a product of the influence of power and politics; the framing and reinforcement of rule systems have been described as being predominantly influenced by 'elites' within the organization (Burns & Dietz, 1992; Nutt, 1993b). Rule systems are viewed as sensitive to context, and responsive to power dynamics within organizations (Nelson & Winter, 2002). Rule systems can also be means of legitimizing asymmetric distributions of power (Cohen et al., 1996). Understanding the decision making environment within an organization therefore requires an appreciation of the political environment (Cohen et al., 1996; Eisenhardt & Bourgeois, 1988; Fredrickson, 1986; Mintzberg et al., 1976).

This study was designed to explore how power is exercised in particular within the context of project initiation decisions, and how it shapes the perceptions and actions of those involved in the initiation process.

UNDERSTANDING THE INFLUENCE OF PERSONALITY ON PROJECT INITIATION

Personality has been identified in a number of contexts as influencing how decision makers approach their roles. In the project management literature, for example, Muller et al. (2009) highlight differences in decision making style of project managers as being attributable to personality. In the decision making literature, it has been suggested that in environments where there are multiple levels of self-interest, decision makers need a clear sense of their objectives, which are in part influenced by their personal preferences (March, 1987). Bourgeois & Eisenhardt (1988; Eisenhardt & Bourgeois, 1988) observe influences of personality as well as politics in the decision making behaviour of executive teams. Personality and preferences of the decision maker have also been observed to have an influence on how the individual makes decisions (Nutt, 1993a). Lastly, Langley et al. (1995) highlight the exploration of differences among decision makers as an area neglected in the literature, calling for research exploring the influence of different types of personalities on decision making.

This study was intended in part to seek to understand how personality contributes to the actions and decisions of those involved in the project initiation process.

UNDERSTANDING THE INFLUENCE OF RULES ON PROJECT INITIATION

Evolutionary principles were introduced to sociology in order to develop a theory of 'the firm' that was consistent with historical analysis and actual observed patterns of behaviour, and it was here that rule following as a decision making concept emerged (Nelson & Winter, 1973). The assumption that firms have 'decision rules', which are retained or replaced through satisficing, provides a basis for both stability where the rules are seen as appropriate and evolution when they are no longer effective (Winter, 1971). Proponents argue that strategic decision processes are rooted in patterns of behaviour that are understood and visible at the executive level of the firm, and provide stability in the face of turnover and the behaviours of individual actors (Fredrickson & Mitchell, 1984). Eisenhardt (1989b) argued that these routines reflect recurring patterns among executives that profoundly influence strategic decision making, and ultimately firm performance. They also have the potential to embed ideologies, which can at extremes substitute for actual decisions (Brunsson, 1982), and result in actors behaving in ways which are unreflective and nonadaptive (Starbuck, 1983).

Overall, however, rules provide a useful lens to understand decision making as an interaction of individual and system influences, where decision rules are a product of power, social interactions and material conditions (Burns & Dietz, 1992). As a result, decision making rules also allow for the exploration of agency, and the degree to which actors perceive flexibility and room to act within the rule system (Dietz & Burns, 1992). Decision rules would appear to provide a useful perspective in understanding the integration between strategy and project, an understanding of politics and a means of exploring the lived experiences of those making initiation decisions.

In the project management literature, it has been suggested that heuristics and biases operating outside the awareness of the decision maker can still have significant influences on how decisions are made (McCray et al., 2002). The broader organizational culture is also seen to influence decision making, highlighting the importance of context in understanding how rules are shaped (Andersen et al., 2009). As suggested above, organizational decision rules are seen to play an important role in both establishing and maintaining the contextual influences that shape decisions (Burns & Dietz, 1992; Dietz & Burns, 1992; Winter, 1971). The study of rule systems provides a greater contextual understanding within which to explore the dynamics of organizations (Nelson & Winter, 2002).

This study endeavours to explore the project initiation process through an examination of the rules systems that are at work within organizations, and an investigation into how these systems are perceived by those involved with initiation decisions, and how they interact with them.

Exploring the Influences on Initiation

The primary intent of the research study presented in this book was to formulate a theory of personal influences on project initiation decisions, which was initially conceived as gaining understanding into how power, personality and rules come together to shape personal involvement in the project initiation process. In the development of substantive theory, the theory is the project of the research; it is not conceived in advance (Corbin & Strauss, 2008; Creswell, 1998).

In this case, while the original research questions were formulated on the basis of reviewing what was already known in the literature about decision making in general and project management in particular, conducting the interviews and analysing the results led to insights into the critical influences of individuals on project initiation decisions. The development of these observations resulted in a shift in emphasis of the study. The analysis provided additional insights and direction that proved to be important in developing a full understanding of project initiation involvement.

Specifically, the original research questions had been based upon an expectation that emerged from the literature that power, personality and rules would be present in equal measure in the project initiation process. While each of these concepts was present, they were operationalized at very different conceptual levels and with different implications for the results. Also, while the findings did provide insights regarding the roles of participants, broader insights in terms of rules and process also emerged. In particular, 'agency' emerged as a particularly influential concept that was central to the study, rather than being a tangential consideration within the larger exploration of rules.

The result of this research is the development of a substantive theory of the influence of agency and rule effectiveness on how project initiation decisions are made in organizations. 'Agency' emerged as the core category that served as the basis of developing this theory; the concept of agency is one that was present in each participant description, whether it was actively influencing decision results, being constrained by process, augmenting rules, or proving perceptually unattainable by participants. The exercise of agency augmented the rule systems of the organizations, whether they were based upon explicitly defined process or implicitly understood conventions.

The findings of this study are that agency is influenced by position, decision involvement and personality. Process effectiveness is influenced by process formality, process consistency, decision process clarity and an emphasis on the process aspects of personal influence. Rule effectiveness is influenced by an emphasis on the political aspects of personal influence, and is negatively impacted by the presence of dysfunctional politics in the decision process and when the role of the project shaper is informal.

The results of this research provide a number of important insights in how we think about getting strategically important projects underway in organizations:

- For those responsible for shaping and championing the initiation of projects, there is a need to understand the dynamics and structures at work in the organization and their own personal ability to influence decision outcomes. Depending upon the environment, there are processes and political forces that can help or hinder them. Equally important, however, is their own personal approach to the role of being a project champion. How they view their role, and the actions that they choose to take, can work to augment the effectiveness of organizational influences. At times, individual influences can support effective decisions even in environments that are otherwise chaotic or dysfunctional.

- For executives actually making ultimate project initiation decisions, it is important to understand the critical roles they play in creating an environment where effective decisions can be made. This includes recognizing when organizational forces work counter to good initiation decisions, and how they can help to better influence the creation of a more effective project initiation environment. At the same time, it is necessary to maintain a clear-eyed understanding of the influences at play in initiation decisions, and how projects are presented in order to be seen in the most favourable possible light.

- Finally, given the range of practices that have been observed – from the effective to the ineffective, from the functional to the dysfunctional – there are many opportunities to improve the process of how project initiation decisions are made. For executive teams and organizational change agents, it is essential to understand the necessary ingredients in creating an environment where better project initiation decisions are possible. It is necessary to appreciate the characteristics of an effective decision making environment, the indicators of dysfunctional behaviours, and the strategies that support consistent, appropriate initiation of the projects most critical to the success of the organization.

A Guide to the Book

This book presents the results of a study that explores the influence of agency and rule effectiveness on project initiation decisions.[1] It presents the results of the research, but also endeavours to provide practical guidance based on the research results.

---

1   Case study numbers are listed in Table 3.4, page 42 and are given in parentheses after quotations.

In particular, it seeks to provide guidance to project shapers, approving executives and those responsible for how initiation decisions are made. It seeks to help identify how individuals and organizations can best support ensuring that project initiation decisions are effective and best support the priorities of the organization.

This chapter has endeavoured to provide an introduction to the role and importance of project initiation decisions in organizational strategies, and what we know and don't know about how initiation decisions get made. This includes an attempt to synthesize a massive literature on decision making (and a moderately sized literature on project management) into a very few readable pages that actually mean something.

Chapter 2 provides a discussion of the challenges of the project initiation process to date. This includes a discussion of how individuals currently attempt to influence project initiation, how the role of 'project shaper' is perceived to support this process, and how decisions do (and don't) get made to initiate projects. In essence, this chapter frames the problem the book is trying to solve.

Chapter 3 is an exploration of what actually influences project decisions. This chapter outlines the theory that emerged from the research study this book is based on, and the role that process, politics and individual agency play in getting project initiation decisions made. It lays out the big picture of how project initiation decisions are made, explaining what the moving parts in the theory are, and why they actually move that way.

Chapter 4 explores the influences of process on project initiation decisions. Process is supposed to play a big role in project initiation decisions. To an extent, there is a role for process, but it is far less prevalent than many maintain. When it works, it works well, and this chapter explores the few examples where this is the case.

Chapter 5 explores the influence of politics on project initiation decisions. Politics is a much more prevalent influence on project initiation decisions. When there are political influences, however, they work in very different (and at times contrary) ways from the way that process works. Politics is not always as predictable or streamlined as process, which is perhaps unsurprising, but because of that, it is not always as effective. This chapter explores the many examples of how politics influences choices.

Chapter 6 explores the influence of individuals in supporting project initiation decisions. Individuals shape the process of project initiation decisions more than many would suggest. While individuals have less influence in truly process-driven environments, they can compensate for organizational inadequacies in politically driven organizations and are the only way things happen in truly dysfunctional organizations. This chapter identifies how individuals are able to exercise influence in their roles, and the dimensions they draw on to be effective.

Chapter 7 explores what happens when project initiation decisions fall apart. Some organizations have very little in place that actually helps projects to be initiated effectively. In these situations, any projects that are initiated get started despite, rather than because of, the organization. Even individual influence can be constrained, diminished and drowned by the influences of organizations with genuinely ineffective environments. This chapter explores just how dysfunctional organizations can actually become.

Chapter 8 provides support and guidance to project shapers about how to approach their role more effectively. For individuals who are trying to get a project initiated, this chapter brings together all the findings of the study to provide a roadmap for how to perform their role effectively. It provides guidance on how to assess the organizational environment, how to understand their role and influence within the environment, and strategies to most effectively shape and influence the project initiation process.

Chapter 9 provides guidance for executives who are responsible for evaluating projects and making the actual decisions about whether or not to proceed. This chapter highlights the influences that conspire to shape how project information is presented. To the extent that the champion plays a role of 'project shaper', the approving executive is the individual whose perceptions they are trying to shape. This chapter provides executives with strategies to develop a clear-eyed understanding of the influences at play, and how projects are presented in order to be seen in the most favourable possible light. The chapter provides guidance on what to look out for, what to avoid, and what questions to ask to make sure they are making the best decision possible.

Chapter 10 concludes the book by providing guidance on how to improve the effectiveness of project initiation decision making within organizations. Given the range of practices that have been observed – from the effective to the ineffective, from the functional to the dysfunctional – there are many opportunities to improve the process of how project initiation decisions are made. This chapter synthesizes what has been presented earlier in the book in order to make recommendations as to how organizations and executive teams can ensure that the projects they *do* initiate are the ones they *should* initiate.

Chapter 2
Exploring How Projects Do (and Don't) Get Initiated

Introduction

When I began the research this book is based upon, it was with the intent to explore how individuals are involved as participants within the project initiation process. Based upon insights gained from prior research, there was a presumption that there would be an influence from power, personality and rules in defining how project initiation decisions are made. It was also presumed that these dimensions had equal stature and would have broadly similar levels of emphasis. In undertaking the research, however, the results revealed very different conceptual implications than had been anticipated at the outset. Firstly, the constructs of power, personality and rules – while present – arose at very different conceptual levels than had been anticipated, with varying degrees of influence on the results. Secondly, the results provided perceptions that went beyond the roles of participants, and led to an awareness that process, rule and decision effectiveness had much larger implications than originally envisioned. Finally, the concept of agency – originally viewed as a tangential offshoot of the larger exploration of rules – emerged within the study as a central and important concept. As a result, the direction of the research, and in particular the research questions at the focus of the analysis, shifted. While the overall focus of the study retained its intent and purpose, the specific questions that it sought to answer evolved.

The Challenges of Project Initiation

As detailed in Chapter 1, there are a number of perspectives as well as many unresolved challenges in how decisions are made within projects, as well as about which projects to undertake. In particular, the influences of social forces, politics and power are significant in understanding how decisions are made. While these areas are only broadly understood in the context of the project management literature, they have been extensively explored in the broader literature of decision making. Understanding these influences and how organizational actors manage them in supporting project initiation is important to understanding how strategy shapes projects, and how projects respond to strategy.

INTEGRATING INITIATION WITH PSYCHOLOGICAL AND POLITICAL FORCES

One of the challenges that must be understood in exploring project initiation decisions is the manner in which inappropriate projects still get initiated. The underlying factors that influence irrational, unwarranted or subjective project initiation decisions are numerous. Flyvbjerg et al. (2009) suggest that delusions and deception are complementary, rather than alternative, explanations; delusions include susceptibility to the planning fallacy and issues of anchoring and adjustment, while deceptions include principal-agent problems in which actors use self-interest, asymmetric information and different risk preferences as tools of deceit to win or keep business. Other studies identify issues related to a lack of clear strategy, where problems at the project level are a product of board-level actors failing to provide clear policy and priorities (for example, Maylor, 2001). Still others suggest much deeper levels of deception, in which the effort of initiating projects provides ample opportunity for actors to make claims and evince convictions to which they do not necessarily adhere, to demand certainty in the face of the unknown, and to use uncertainty as a way of manufacturing political hypocrisy (for example, van Marrewijk et al., 2008). Clearly, any understanding of project initiation decisions needs to specifically accommodate the possibility of deception, negligence or manipulation.

Strategies to remove or manage these biases include the introduction of reference class forecasting as a means of comparing projects with others that are similar in order to validate estimates of cost and benefit; this strategy is based upon the assumption that 'ventures are typically more similar than actors assume, even ventures that on the surface of things may appear entirely different' (Flyvbjerg, 2008, p. 8). Attempting to address political influences of deception have thus far resulted in observations that the power relations governing estimation and project initiation themselves need to change; greater transparency and accountability must be introduced into the project initiation process (Flyvbjerg, 2009).

The challenge in supporting project initiation is to develop approaches that actually enable the adoption of such transparency and accountability.

INTEGRATING INITIATION WITH STRATEGIC MANAGEMENT

To address the challenges associated with understanding the influences of strategy on making project initiation decision requires that it be situated within the larger context of the strategic management of the organization, and also requires that the dynamics of the decision making processes be explored. For some, project management has been (or should have been) long considered a part of the strategic management domain: 'The art and skills of project management reach right into the earliest stages of project initiation' (Morris, 1989, p. 184). Research perspectives have positioned projects as largely responsive to the deliberate formulations that emerge from the strategic management process of the organization, while still needing to accommodate more emergent notions of strategy (Artto et al., 2008; Vuori et al., 2012). Other perspectives view business projects as 'strategic interventions' that influence the overall process of strategic management as means of influencing business change (for example, Winter et al., 2006). Still others place the project initiation decision, and the role of projects, in a more entrepreneurial context that positions projects as both related to and yet autonomous from the larger organization (Lindgren & Packendorff, 2009; Vuori et al., 2012). While identifying the need to integrate with project strategy is easy, adopting strategies to actually do so is considerably more complex.

Approaches to improving the integration of project initiation with organizational strategy include reframing how the idea of project strategy (and organizational strategy) is developed. Proponents suggest the need to establish an alignment between organizational strategy and project strategy (Maylor, 2001; Milosevic & Srivannaboon, 2006; Shenhar, 2001). Others point out the need to allow for a more iterative form of initiation than is standard now, one that enables a more dynamic and interactive evolution of strategy in response to uncertainties (Lehtonen & Martinsuo, 2008). Further investigations have proposed a reframing of the concept of what constitutes 'project strategy' and the nature of how planning progresses in support of organizational strategy (Pitsis et al., 2003). Still other suggestions include the need for explicit recognition of the strategic management processes in organizations as having both deliberate and emergent aspects (Artto et al., 2008; Vuori et al., 2012). While there have been various proposals regarding how to accomplish the integration of projects within strategy, what remains is the need to investigate how this is accomplished in actual practice and to examine the implications of such strategies being adopted within organizations.

ENCOURAGING RESEARCH INTO THE FRONT END OF PROJECTS

While there are some suggestions of solutions and approaches to the inherent political, power, social and psychological challenges associated with project initiation, the limitations and barriers that result from current levels of understanding of these influencing forces are acknowledged in the majority of these discussions. The escalation literature has seen calls for the further study of the dynamics of both escalation and exit, with a particular emphasis on multi-method and multi-level investigations; these specifically suggest that drawing on experimental, archival, questionnaire and case study data would be potentially fruitful (Ross & Staw, 1993). There have been proposals for more investigations of cognitive psychology, investigating how the templates that drive framing, anchoring and optimism biases are formed and utilized; these have also included consideration of cognitive dissonance theory, in which the meaning of decisions is changed by altering the nature of the underlying alternatives (Thomas, 1998). Further study of the causes of psychological bias, and particularly political deception, have also been suggested (Flyvbjerg, 2009). These research proposals in particular emphasize investigating the dynamics of power, politics and influence, rather than the normative and rational process approaches that have dominated much of the literature to date.

Embedded within suggestions for further research has also been the need to better understand the complexity and uncertainty associated with project initiation decisions. Explicitly rational processes are perceived to ignore the existence of subjective rationality, leading to projects being initiated for unclear reasons, with greater emphasis on process than outcomes, and despite changes in the environment rendering objectives obsolete or undesirable (Packendorff, 1995). Initiation decisions are often the products of unclear objectives, devised by stakeholders with conflicting views, where there is a need for advocacy as much as rational analysis (Winter et al., 2006b). While politics and power are operative forces in normal human functioning, arguments are made that this is not necessarily the result of conscious intent or malevolent design as much as it is a product of professionals confronting issues of ambiguity, uncertainty and complexity, and that as a result, issues of power, ambiguity and paradox must be better understood (van Marrewijk et al., 2008). The implication for future research into project initiation is that there is a need to navigate a complex web of dynamics that integrate influences of politics, power, ambiguity, uncertainty and complexity with the motivations and limitations of individual actors.

Individual Influences on Project Initiation

It is perhaps helpful at this point to explore why it is so important to explore how individual actors approach the project initiation process. Regardless of the structures, processes, rules and guidelines that may be in place, project initiation is ultimately the product of individuals. Ultimately, it is a person who influences – and finally determines – whether a project is going to be initiated. Even where decisions are made in groups, it is rare that they are exclusively made through group processes. Individuals serve as advocates to the group, they chair the group's functioning, and they choose to speak – or not speak – in favour of or against whether a particular project should proceed.

In fact, there are numerous areas where action is influenced by individual actors in the initiation of projects. The process of project initiation is not simply limited to the decision of whether or not to proceed with a project. Similarly, individual actors are not solely involved in making the decision. At the beginning, an idea is advanced that a project should be undertaken. Time is spent investigating and exploring that idea, in order to understand the implications of the project and how the work of the project might be accomplished. Further analysis and investigation explores the impact the project might have on the organization, and the benefits that might or might not be realized. The idea is championed to others in the organization, in order to build awareness of what would be involved and why the project might be important. Support is secured from others, and in particular those who might have power to sway whether or not the project should proceed. Finally, after much effort, some level of agreement – formally or informally – is made to proceed with the project. At each stage, from development of the idea to agreement to proceed, individual actors play a role in advancing the project or opposing it.

Understanding the influences that individuals have on project initiation is not just a question of knowing what happens at the moment of decision. There is a need to understand the forces at work and the influences at play at each stage in the life of the idea. We need to understand how actors perceive their roles, and the means they have available to exercise influence. And we need to understand the organizational forces that enable or constrain those actors in performing those roles. This requires expanding the field being explored beyond the individual, while still keeping the attributes, roles and actions of the individual actor at the forefront of our explorations.

The Role of the Project Shaper

A particularly promising line of enquiry in investigating the path forward in understanding project initiation decisions and the influence of individuals is that of Smith & Winter (2010). Their initial study specifically focused on the 'messy social processes' that lead to projects being proposed and initiated. Not simply a product of rational and normative techniques, this process carries: 'awareness of projects as socially constructed entities. Rather than being pre-existing objects to be subjected to the instrumental techniques of conventional project management, they are created and shaped by individual players in the workplace' (Smith & Winter, 2010, p. 48).

In framing their discussion of project initiation, Smith & Winter (2010) identified six key dimensions that comprise a framework for evaluating how project initiation decisions are shaped:

1.   **The control model of projects** – Viewing project management as having primarily a control focus echoes the observation of numerous other researchers (see, for example, Maylor, 2001; Packendorff, 1995; Söderlund, 2004; Thomas & Tjäder, 2000), Smith & Winter (2010) specifically identified two narrative views of control: that of project management as determining the best and most orderly and efficient route of delivery; and that of project management as a tyranny that destroys autonomy, initiative and creativity. They also raised issues regarding when a project actually becomes a project, with the amusingly relevant warning to 'beware premature projectification' (Smith & Winter, 2010, p. 53).

2.   **Tribal power** – Recognizing projects as social constructions, Smith & Winter (2010) also acknowledge that they are constructed by diverse groups with diverse agendas. Projects therefore need to both acknowledge and consciously address the expectations of this multi-tribal world. This requires that project shapers act as expert players within the social world of tribes, consulting, facilitating and leading towards a unified view of the project. This reinforces the call for project managers to be adaptive experts and reflective practitioners (Cicmil, 2006; Crawford et al., 2006b; Thomas & Mengel, 2008).

3.   **Transformation and value** – Smith & Winter (2010) discuss the need for the project manager to focus on the value of the project,

however that is defined. This builds on calls to revisit and redefine how success is perceived and evaluated (Steffens et al., 2007; Winter et al., 2006a; Winter et al., 2006b).

4.   **Enacted reality** – For projects to be viewed as real and initiated, Smith & Winter (2010) argue for the need to create clarity out of the chaos and complexity of how projects are defined and interpreted: 'Any version of the project scope can be open to challenge as different groups manoeuvre to promote their tribal interests. Project progress, however, requires some degree of stability of purpose, and this is achieved through enactment' (Smith & Winter, 2010, p. 55). Referencing in part the work of Weick (1995), Smith and Winter say that this requires the project manager to act as the sensemaker of the project, as well as demonstrating its reality through co-ordinating the production of artifacts which can be seen, inspected and queried.

5.   **External dynamics: peripety** – Smith & Winter (2010) define 'peripety' as the Aristotelian concept of the plot point in a play where new information transforms our understanding of what happens: 'It is not only the outcomes that are changed, but the questions that frame the project thinking and plans' (Smith & Winter, 2010, p. 55). This concept recognizes that projects are subject to the influence of external forces at different points in their lives, and that expert practitioners will go out of their way to engage with external influencers, and to continue to actively shape perceptions as change emerges.

6.   **Shaper's volition** – 'Volition' is identified by Smith & Winter (2010) as a powerful and significant determinant of the form that a project ultimately takes: 'For each project, the scope becomes what it is because of the strong action of an individual who chooses to shape it in that way' (Smith & Winter, 2010, p. 56). The actions of project shapers are constrained by the forces within the context in which they operate, and by the agendas and motivations of the actors with whom they interact; at the same time, they are enacting their own roles within the organization: 'choosing allegiances, supporting their personal agenda within the organization, protecting their credibility and reputation, and, if failure is on the cards, manoeuvring themselves into a winning position' (Smith & Winter, 2010, p. 56).

The focus of Smith & Winter's exploration of the shaping and forming of projects is on the expertise, wisdom and reflexivity of practitioners. Their operative assumption is that project initiation is less a product of rational and normative functions of gate-keeping and good governance, and more a product of the degree to which those who shape projects are able to operate as reflective, intuitive, pragmatic and ethical players within the organizational contexts in which they operate.

The relevance of the conceptual model proposed by Smith and Winter is that it firmly establishes the role of the project shaper in the project initiation process, and frames that role as one that operates inherently within the social, political and power structures of the organization. Further exploration of the role of shaping projects requires an understanding of the activities and – to the degree it is possible to do so – the motives of the individuals fulfilling this role. Smith & Winter view this as being possible to achieve only through in-depth research into the actuality of projects: 'We hope that the arguments we have set out here, promoting the central role of the project shaper and setting out a framework for understanding the activities of such an individual, can form a basis for such research' (Smith & Winter, 2010, p. 59).

The conceptual model developed by Smith & Winter (2010) would appear to provide a promising perspective from which to investigate project initiation decisions. The current model, however, is the result of a small number of case studies which were reviewed to extrapolate the dimensions that have been proposed. There is no underlying theoretical framework, and no theoretical lens is suggested for its further development. In order to evaluate the degree to which their conceptualization of the role of project shaper is appropriate to the study of project initiation and the dimensions which they discuss are relevant, it will be necessary to establish a firm theoretical foundation.

Influences on Project Initiation

In conducting this study, there was a need to explore comprehensively how participants perceived the process of making project initiation decisions, and what factors were perceived as influencing process and decision effectiveness. While exploring this issue, it was my hope to develop a basis for understanding what factors influence the effectiveness of decision making processes, and the influences of individuals in supporting these processes. This section provides an overview of the initial findings that emerged from the research, as illustrated in Figure 2.1. In particular, it highlights the initial categories of influence that were found to be significant in shaping the project initiation decision, and the effectiveness of the decision making process.

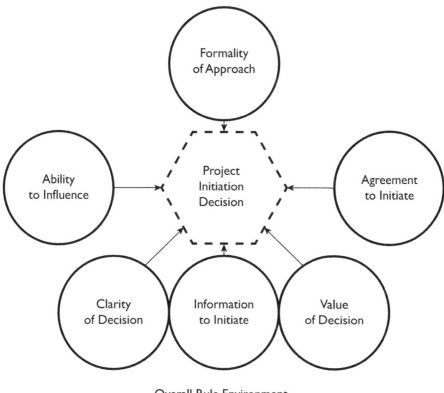

Figure 2.1   Initial categories of analysis

The following points provide an overview of the purpose and intent of each of the initial categories:

- **ability to influence** – the degree of influence and latitude the participants have in the project initiation process, and consideration of the other influences that may be required at a sponsor or executive level to ensure initiation;

- **agreement to initiate** – the degree to which there is actually agreement within the organization to initiate a project, including definition of the decision making process and the degree to which a decision is recognized by the participant as having been made;

- **formality of approach** – the relative formality of the process supporting project initiation, including the consistency of the process and the formality of the documentation produced within the process;

- **clarity of decision** – the degree to which the results of the decision process are clear, understandable and aligned with the direction of the organization;

- **information to initiate** – an understanding of the information that needs to be identified and considered as input prior to making the decision;

- **value of decision** – the degree to which the value of the potential results of a project is considered as part of the initiation process;

- **overall rule environment** – the underlying rule environment within the organization that supports and enables the project initiation process, including the consistency and stability of the rules regarding project initiation and the degree to which they are explicit or implicit.

Each of these dimensions of influence is described in further detail below, in order to provide a more comprehensive understanding of the essential concepts that emerged in conducting the research. In order to protect confidentiality, each quotation from a participant will be identified by a case number in parentheses.

ABILITY TO INFLUENCE

The concept of 'ability to influence' explores the degree of influence and the role that participants have in the decision making process with respect to initiating projects. For the majority of participants, their role was to provide input into the process. Often, this was in the form of developing documentation or preparing analyses for consideration by others in making project initiation decisions. A smaller number of participants indicated that they would either participate in the decision making process directly, or make recommendations. Those who participated were typically members of the executive team within their organization, and as a result of their role were involved in the collaborative process of making an initiation decision. Those who recommended decisions were more likely to do so because of their seniority in the organization, or their participation in a team whose responsibility was to make recommendations that would be forwarded to a subsequent decision making body. Interestingly, only one participant in the research was actually the final decision maker in the project initiation process; while many participants had high levels of seniority, and several were members of their organization's executive team, no other participant had sufficient autonomy to make initiation decisions in isolation. By contrast, two participants indicated that they had no influence on the decision making that led to projects being initiated. Characterizing their involvement, one participant indicated: 'We pick them up once we inherit them. At what stage? It runs the gamut; we have started a project, and now we need a project manager. We don't start projects, we catch up to them' (11). Perhaps most interestingly, a number of participants who perceived their actual influence on the project initiation process to be comparatively low were often identified as being at relatively senior levels in their organizations. While all participants were involved in some degree in the decision making process, the degree of influence was often – although not always – related to the seniority of the participant in their organization.

The means participants drew upon in exercising their influence also varied. The exercise of influence reflected the means by which participants established their credibility and impact in supporting the project initiation process. Some participants established influence through an emphasis on process, identifying the importance of diligence, experience and past performance, and ensuring adherence to process. Others established influence through political savvy, relationships, proactive communication and the leveraging of power through position and delegation. Most interestingly, the influences participants highlighted tended to emphasize one driver or another: participants would indicate a tendency to leverage politics or process to gain influence, but not both.

Returning to the discussion of the project shaper in Smith & Winter (2010), every participant indicated that the role of project shaper existed within their organization to some degree. For several participants, the role was identified as being present, but highly informal in nature. For most organizations, the role was an individual's; in half of the organizations, it was identified as being the role of the sponsor, while for a few it was defined as the role of the project manager. Success in this role strongly relies on credibility, which numerous participants identified as being a challenge: 'Sometimes that person isn't strong enough to do that role – confident, capable. Part of the challenge is to get the person to that level. Where they can be a voice for the staff' (5). Even though the role of project shaper was viewed as being prevalent, the capability and influence of the person in that role had a significant influence on their success, and the ability to effectively advocate for projects.

In addition to the shaper role, participants also frequently discussed the role of the project sponsor. The vast majority of participants identified the need for a champion who was responsible for ownership of the project. At times this role overlapped with the idea of a project shaper, and in other contexts it reflected a larger responsibility for on-going business ownership: 'When I come back to the sponsor piece, you have to have a sponsor who is engaged and driving and who is leading and is providing the support and removing the hurdles' (3). Nearly half of all participants viewed the role of sponsor as needing to be held at the executive level, while in some instances the actual exercising of the responsibilities associated with the role was varied. Sponsorship can also be viewed as varying depending upon the importance of the project or the skills of the person in the role, while a few participants specifically highlighted weak sponsorship as being a challenge in their organizations. While sponsorship was identified as being of critical importance by the majority of participants, there were several instances where it was inadequate, and its alignment with what participants described as the role of shaper was not always clear.

AGREEMENT TO INITIATE

The dimension of 'agreement to initiate' reflects the degree to which there is established agreement within the organization that the project should proceed. This includes understanding the process by which agreement is established, and the degree to which agreement is actually formally recognized. In particular, the degree of formality underlying the decision making process varied considerably. For a few organizations, the decision was inferred; in other words, because activity was happening on a project, there was a belief that somewhere, someone had made a decision to conduct the project. Perhaps surprisingly, the vast majority of project initiation decisions were the result of verbal commitments: 'Ultimately, the decision won't be made in presentation – they will sit on it a little bit, they will talk it over amongst themselves, and then a week or so later they will announce a decision' (19). Only a small number of organizations actually described an initiation process that included a formal sign-off on the project initiation decision. In a small number of organizations, there was no formality whatsoever: 'Not even great decision tracking, or even writing decisions down' (2). For the majority of participants, decisions were recognized as occurring, but those decisions were often perceived as being quite informal.

The influence of politics on making an initiation decision was discussed in detail by virtually all participants. In a significant majority of the cases, politics was identified as having a strong influence on the decision making process. The participants described politics as being: 'absolutely huge. Worse on some, but absolutely in all' (22). In half of all cases, politics was critical in ensuring buy-in and support for project initiation activities. Depending upon the participant, political activities could be seen as being positive or negative. A number of participants identified a political environment characterized by disagreement and discord, while several others characterized the political culture as constructive. The culture of the organization influenced the political environment for many organizations, and while sometimes positive, the culture was also often described as being characterized by avoidance, where there was a: 'mostly risk-averse culture – it doesn't deal with outright confrontation. We will sheepishly address them. And they will do it again next time' (13). In only a very small number of organizations was politics not identified as having an influence; these individuals identified the process of project initiation as having more influence than the political discussions that surrounded it. While politics was described as being critical to the process of project initiation, how politics emerged differed radically among the participant organizations.

A key aspect underlying the category of 'agreement to initiate' is the degree to which decision recognition exists – an appreciation that a decision has been made, and awareness of what the implications of that decision actually represent. For a few organizations, the process of initiation and project planning were intertwined, where initiation: 'starts with the development of the project charter and the project plan, and ends with sign-off' (3). For a significant number of organizations, the initiation process was the planning process; people were told to go and do a project, and the very first activity was building a project plan. Only a small number of participants indicated a situation where the initiation process was formally separate and distinct from that of project planning. In a few instances, it was the structure imposed by a project management office that drove this formality, and for others formal initiation as a separate and distinct process was embedded within their defined processes. The result was that while projects were initiated, many of the processes were informal and indistinct, and frequently the decision, while made, was indicated by verbal direction rather than formal sign-off.

FORMALITY OF APPROACH

The dimension of 'formality of approach' asks the specific question of how formally the process of project initiation is actually managed. What constitutes the formal documentation required to initiate a project was a particular point of variation, with participants indicating that they would be required to produce a detailed business case, a high-level business case, a project charter or a project plan. Some organizations described an approach that was less reliant on documentation and more focused on discussion, basing initiation decisions on presentations. For a few participants, an extremely high-level summary document would suffice: 'Does that look like a charter? Unless it is just an IT project, I am not seeing charters used a lot. We don't have a lot of pure [project management]-type practices. Would look like a two-page document' (16). While the majority of participants described some level of documentation, the formality and detail were subject to a great deal of variation, and few participants described initiation documents that aligned with formal project management or strategy practices.

There was also a considerable degree of variation in terms of process consistency. This describes how often the process of project initiation is managed the same way within the organization. The majority of participants indicated that the process of project initiation had moderate consistency, and described their organization's environment as one in which the process: 'sometimes varies. A lot of times it is driven by how urgent the initiative has to be implemented, how large it is, what part of the organization is running with it' (21). A few participants indicated that the process was mostly consistent or very consistent, but an equal number indicated that the process was very inconsistent. One perspective on this indicated: 'We struggle with this. Before charter stage, there is not a consistent way of getting from an idea to an official project charter' (2). The degree of consistency varied greatly in the participant descriptions, from completely lacking to extremely rigorous.

In addition to questions of consistency, there are also questions regarding formality of the initiation process for projects. Approximately half of the participants described an environment where there was no formal process for project initiation. At the same time, there were instances where the presence of a process had no impact on actual practice: 'We don't tend to not approve projects. Not a lot projects don't get approved. We have a tendency to approve more projects than we can actually deliver. That tends to be our primary problem' (1). While a significant number of participants indicated some formality regarding the project initiation process, this reflected a range of challenges, including processes still in development, processes that existed but were not well applied, processes that were flexible, and processes that, while being adhered to, did not actually produce relevant decisions. Only a small number of participants indicated that a relatively formal process of project initiation was in place. For the majority of participants, even the presence of a process did not result in consistent usage, and the actual decision making activities were often very informal.

Given the lack of formality, the question of process effectiveness was very important for participants. Nearly half of all participants described an initiation environment where the process was ineffective. For some, this was the result of not having an identifiable process. Others indicated that there was a process, but that it was not used. According to one participant: 'We have a very clearly defined process that we put in place shortly after joining the organization; it probably lasted about three months, and then got thrown out the window. Tried to revitalize the process earlier this year; not a lot of success' (7). A few indicated that their process didn't actually result in prioritization decisions, and some also indicated that the results of the process were not understood or trusted. Most of the other participants indicated that their initiation process was only somewhat effective. This was the result of inconsistency, lack of adherence, differing processes being applied to different projects, little control actually being imposed on initiation or the process being too new to have an impact. Some spoke of challenges being introduced through compromises being imposed by the initiation process: 'I worry about that. Will I have to compromise too much? Will I lose benefits that the organization may want to achieve? Will we compromise user experience because of demands for other features?' (22). Only a very small number of organizations described the presence of a very effective process. This is significant, in that while all participants recognized project initiation processes, the vast majority indicated that the one at their organization was not effective or was only moderately effective in supporting the actual initiation of projects.

CLARITY OF DECISION

The dimension of 'clarity of decision' explores the degree to which the result of the initiation process is a clear path forward in terms of what has been committed to. Only a few participants indicated that the project initiation process resulted in a clear plan. Half of the participants indicated that the initiation process resulted in a general direction, and a smaller subset suggested that the result of the initiation process was an inferred solution: 'They would finalize it – get it under way probably without understanding what the scope implied as far as things like how it should be architected would go. Everyone would nod and agree and start marching' (23). A small subset of participants indicated that the initiation process in their organization was unworkable or resulted in a tendency to defer decisions until more information was available:

'We have had instances where hard decisions have had to be made and have required trade-offs, and those decisions tend to get deferred as well' (1). Many participant descriptions indicated that projects at the time of initiation were not developed to an extent where the organization had a clear picture of the results it intended to obtain.

Another significant and problematic area was the degree to which decisions to initiate projects were aligned with the strategic direction of the organization. A large number of participants indicated that projects were matched to strategy in the project initiation process, meaning that as projects were identified, they were justified retroactively in terms of how they related to a predefined strategy: 'I suppose they all consider the larger government mandate. Does this fit in the government business plan? Which priorities does this assist with? Doesn't go much beyond that' (4). Only a small number of participants indicated that strategy drove project initiation choices, and a few also indicated that there was a presumed link to the strategic plan for initiated projects. More than half of all participants indicated that the initiation process was predominantly reactive to demands, and several more suggested the process was ad hoc: 'Decisions get made on a whimsy – it depends upon the mood what gets initiated' (1). While participants described a theoretical alignment with strategy within many organizations, very few projects seemed to be initiated with a conscious alignment to organizational strategy.

INFORMATION TO INITIATE

The dimension of 'decision information' identifies the information that is required and considered during the project initiation process. This includes information contained within formal documents and deliverables as well as informally compiled or assessed information. Respondents demonstrated a comprehensive and diverse number of perspectives on what is required in terms of information to support project initiation. Participants identified the need to understand background, understand goals, understand impacts, understand lessons learned on previous projects, understand success and define approach. The need to research alternatives was also identified, as well as the need to present external benchmarks, and the need to consider change management as part of the initiation process. While this suggests a relative degree of formality in the analysis and consolidation of information, a number of stakeholders still indicated that they wanted more analysis of projects prior to initiation:

We do talk a lot about wanting to do a lot of analysis. In terms of actual time, we take on too many projects as a group. We find that we tend to do less analysis than we should. We are pressured to complete existing projects. We are not always spending enough time at the analysis stage. (26)

In short, many participants did not consider the analysis undertaken sufficient.

Respondents' perceptions of failure to conduct sufficient analysis were supplemented by their statements that the level and detail of analysis varied depending upon the type of project being conducted. A number of participants suggested that rigour depended upon the purpose, and more than half suggested that rigour depended upon the project type. Relative perceived urgency was also an influence. Such comments suggested that different decision makers within the organizations had different degrees of expectation regarding the information required in choosing to proceed with projects.

What information was actually sought varied by respondent as well. Some participants sought their own understanding, while a few participants relied on the views of others in determining the viability of a project initiation decision: 'Apart from the knowledge that we bring to the table, we don't do our own kind of investigation. At least I don't. I rely on the information in the proposal, and the presenter' (4). More than half of participants indicated that despite the analysis and information that might be assembled, there was a tendency within their organization to commit to a solution prematurely, and a number of other participants suggested that any analysis tended to get overridden by executive imperatives. A significant challenge was the sense that any analysis only served to justify a pre-ordained conclusion, with documentation primarily serving to justify decisions that had already been made. For many participants, the effort to compile analysis and demonstrate rigour appeared to be more an issue of justification than a product of considered deliberation.

VALUE OF DECISION

The dimension of 'value of decision' identifies the means by which the value of potential projects is considered within the project initiation process. This includes the degree to which the value of a project is formally defined and articulated prior to project initiation, and the degree to which tangible and intangible factors influence the assessment of potential value. While respondents indicated that in their organizations there was a fairly broad discussion of overall analysis as part of the project initiation process, there was much less emphasis on understanding the value of potential projects. While some participants indicated that value was formally defined and evaluated, a comparable number indicated that value was informally considered or inconsistent:

> *It is probably too finite to say it is just retail projects, but more where projects are customer facing, there tends to be not a lot of scrutiny. That tends to be in the main retail projects. Compliance projects which are a cost burden face a great deal of scrutiny. (1)*

For several organizations, value was not considered in any manner as part of the project initiation process. Participants appeared to place much less emphasis on considerations of value in determining whether to proceed with projects.

Where value was assessed, perspectives differed on the nature of value that had to be demonstrated. A significant number of participants indicated that any demonstration of value needed to be tangible and quantifiable. While a number of other participants allowed for the role and importance of intangible dimensions of value, it was rare that this was the primary area of emphasis. For some participants, value itself was reframed, with four participants indicating that the primary emphasis was on being 'cost-sensitive'. This perspective is demonstrated by the comment: 'if I view this from [our] standpoint, we have been sort of there a couple of times, when we have come to an understanding of the cost, there is usually a quick backing away from it' (19). Measures of value appear to have been regarded with scepticism by many participants, and even projects with good promise were dismissed if the costs were considered too high.

OVERALL RULE ENVIRONMENT

The dimension of 'overall rule environment' encompasses the system of rules that are employed in governing the project initiation process within organizations. A particular area of consideration, and one that we will explore in considerable detail later, is the idea of decision agency, or the degree of flexibility and freedom that participants had to work within the organization to support project initiation. Several participants indicated that they had no flexibility in working within the rule system; rule adherence was essentially mandatory. For some, this was the result of the rigidity of process; for others, it was predominantly a result of the political environment within their organizations. In reference to organizational rules, one participant indicated: 'Probably, I stub my toe once a week on one I didn't know about' (23). More than half of participants indicated that they had some flexibility in terms of adhering to and working with the rules of their organization – usually because there was some degree of process that they were required to adhere to, and because they recognized others who had political influence over the final project initiation decision. Only a small number of participants indicated that they had 'considerable flexibility' in working within the rule environments of their organizations: 'Figured out how to work within this culture. It is a relationship-driven organization – if you have the relationship, that is how things get done: Through the back door conversations' (16). There was a broad spectrum of responses from participants, from those willing to work around the rules to those that worked strictly within them.

A variety of 'explicit rules' were in place to govern the initiation of projects. For a small subset of participants, the explicit rules were clearly defined, with this clarity being a response to political issues, an espoused expectation or simply a reflection of how projects are actually initiated. By contrast, a number of participants indicated that there were minimal explicit rules within their organization. The underlying themes for this were diverse, and included comments about rules being limited to the expectation of a business case, or the definition of a project, or the commitment that a formal decision would in fact be made. In addition, participants indicated that there were minimal practices, minimal compliance and only general alignment of the rules with overall direction. Finally, a small number of participants indicated that there were no explicit rules within their organization governing project initiation, despite their perceived importance: 'Very important. You need a common field of play so that everyone understands what it is that they need to be providing. If we are going to start evaluating one project against another, [we] need a common understanding' (8). In all, surprisingly few organizations appeared to have clearly defined explicit rules in place relating to project initiation, and there was a great deal of room for interpretation and movement.

Participants outlined a broad array of implicit rules regarding the process of project initiation. One of the implicit rules discussed was that process has value; several participants suggested that there was an implicit appreciation of process within their organization, either because of the perception of value associated with having a process, because experts were responsible for the process, or because the process was in fact being adhered to. For some participants, process was implicit; while it was not articulated or written down, it was understood.

> *The pitfall is, I understand the rules in my own head, but sometimes they don't get conveyed. Sometimes the problem is that the rules are my rules, and they haven't been formally adopted within the organization or in the PMO – part of the vision that I have that hasn't really made its way out yet. (3)*

There was a much broader implicit understanding of politics, with more than half of the participants highlighting the implications of politics on project initiation; in this context, there was discussion of the need to leverage relationships, exercise influence and work within the culture. Overall, participant responses suggested that implicit rules had a broader and more comprehensive influence on project initiation than explicit rules do.

An important consideration in understanding the rule environment within organizations was the idea of rule consistency: the degree to which the rules as understood (whether implicit or explicit) were actually adhered to. The majority of participants reported that the rules within their organization were inconsistent, reasons for this including cultural differences, inconsistent expectations, silo influences, the existence of multiple processes, political influences, avoidance of processes, and a lack of history within the organization. Only a few participants indicated some consistency in their rule systems; they felt this was due to a conscious desire to remain flexible, a greater emphasis on implicit rules within the organization, or consistency being limited to only some aspects of the process. Finally, a small number of participants indicated that the rule system in their organization was very consistent; in all cases, these organizations had a strong explicit process environment in place: 'We are very stringent – some might say over the top – but because we are in audit and tax, we have to be' (20). These results suggest that not only were there fewer organizations described as having an explicit rather than an implicit process, but even where they were present, the application of explicit rules was low, except in a much smaller subset of organizations.

Lastly, the idea of rule effectiveness explores the degree to which the rule system in place helped in providing good project initiation decisions. According to the majority of participants, the rule system currently in place was not effective. Reasons for this included: there was no rule system in place; the rule system that was defined was not used or was subverted; the rule system was not fully articulated or understood, or the system did not produce decisions that were considered effective. Several more participants indicated that the rule system was only somewhat effective in their organizations. They suggested that this was due to: a lack of full awareness of the rule system within the organization; the evolving nature of the rule system; political influences on how the rules were applied; differences between explicit and implicit rules, and/or excess scrutiny of projects within the organization. By way of illustration, one participant said: 'If the explicit rules are followed then a number of tasks have been completed prior to the [project manager] being assigned. If the implicit rules are followed in initiation, then the tasks the [project manager] needs to perform would vary' (21). Only a very small number of participants indicated that the rule systems in their organizations were very effective. One of these said: 'Very stable. Very repeatable. It's the business we are in' (28). These results suggest that for many organizations, the rule systems that were in place governing project initiation were not being used, or were being complied with only to the degree that there was scrutiny, and as a result were often being worked around. It is interesting to note that only a few participants felt that the rules that were in place were appropriate and effective.

Conclusions

The participant inputs described above exhibit a diversity of practices in project initiation, in a broad array of organizations. Participants did not tell the same story over and over again; their responses showed that very different approaches were applied in different organizations, with varying levels of formality and consistency. Some practices were written down, while others were only generally understood. A small number of participants saw the process of project initiation as being very clear, very formal and very much adhered to in their organizations, while another subset suggested that there were no rules about how projects were initiated, and that the presence of some rules might go a long way toward helping the organization to improve how it made project initiation decisions.

While the diversity of findings is interesting, they are not overly helpful or instructive when viewed in isolation. In particular, they do not provide a real insight into how decision making practices interact to produce effective – or ineffective – project initiation decisions. Determining the factors that led to effective decisions, and considering those aspects that led to ineffective decisions, required a great deal more analysis and the development of additional insight. What emerged from this exploration was the importance of agency in influencing the project initiation process, and the degree to which personal agency intersects with the formal and political rule systems of the organization to determine how decisions are actually made. The results of this analysis are presented in the next chapter.

Chapter 3
The Influences on Project Initiation

Introduction

The research this book is based upon was designed to explore how project initiation decisions are made within organizations. The study particularly focused on the rule systems that govern project initiation decisions and the influences that individual participants in the project initiation decision process have on applying and influencing those rule systems. This was examined through exploring the experiences of the project initiation experiences of participants in a variety of organizations and work environments. The approach to project initiation, and the organizational and individual factors that contributed to this process, was explored in detail. In particular, there was an attempt to understand those factors that were particularly effective, or singularly ineffective, in supporting the journey of an initiative from idea to approved project.

The result is a framework of project initiation that places the agency of participants at the centre of their involvement in the project initiation process. This framework identifies both personal and structural influences, and how these influences interact in supporting the development of project initiation decisions. The framework also supports understanding how individuals are able to exercise influence within the project initiation process. This leads to an overall theory of the influence of agency and rule emphasis on the effectiveness of project initiation decision making.

Introducing the Participants

The participants in this study were drawn predominantly from organizations throughout North America (specifically Canada and the United States), but there were also three international participants (from Australia), as illustrated in Table 3.1.

Table 3.1   Geographic distribution of participants

Country	No. of participants
Canada	19
United States	8
Australia	3

Participants in the study worked in a variety of sectors, and in a range of different industries. Sectors included for-profit, not-for-profit and government/public-sector organizations. Participants self-identified the industries in which they worked as shown in Table 3.2.

Table 3.2   Industry distribution of participants

Industry	No. of participants
Aerospace	1
Consulting	2
Education	9
Finance	4
Government	5
Insurance	3
Mining, oil and gas	2
Pharmaceuticals	1
Professional association	1
Retail	1
Telecommunications	1

While they had all been involved in supporting the project initiation process in some manner, participants reported that they performed various roles within their organizations, as illustrated in Table 3.3.

Table 3.3   Role distribution of participants

Position	No. of participants
Executive	6
Mid-management	14
Project management	10

The profiles described in Tables 3.1–3.3 are not provided in order to suggest that the results of this study will be generalizable to all decision making contexts. At the same time, however, they show that the participants were drawn from a sufficiently broad cross-section of sectors, industries and organizations, with a corresponding variety of project types and roles, that the findings with respect to how project initiation decisions are made should be reasonably representative for the majority of readers of this study.

In conducting this study, every effort was made to keep the findings grounded in the data that was collected, and to present participant experiences in a manner that illustrates and provides contextual richness to the concepts being discussed. At the same time, a central ethical consideration that was addressed in the study design, and that is central to the ethics approval obtained to conduct the study, is that of protecting the confidentiality of individual respondents. As such, all inputs to this study have been anonymized and no information that would enable the identification of organizations or individual participants has been included. Quotations that are included in this book are identified by a case number in parentheses, in order to maintain continuity of understanding while protecting participant confidentiality. Table 3.4 is a summary overview of Tables 3.1–3.3, and provides a broader contextual understanding of the participants.

Table 3.4   Summary overview of case participants

Case no.	Country	Industry	Position
1	Australia	Finance	Mid-management
2	Canada	Government	Mid-management
3	Canada	Government	Executive
4	Canada	Government	Mid-management
5	Canada	Insurance	Mid-management
6	United States	Pharmaceuticals	Mid-management
7	Canada	Insurance	Executive
8	Canada	Government	Executive
9	Canada	Government	Mid-management
10	Canada	Professional association	Executive
11	United States	Education	Mid-management
12	United States	Education	Project manager
13	United States	Education	Project manager
14	United States	Education	Project manager
15	United States	Education	Mid-management
16	Canada	Mining, oil and gas	Mid-management
17	Canada	Mining, oil and gas	Mid-management
18	United States	Aerospace	Mid-management
19	Canada	Retail	Mid-management
20	Canada	Consulting	Mid-management
21	Canada	Finance	Project manager
22	Canada	Education	Executive
23	Canada	Insurance	Project manager
24	Australia	Telecommunications	Project manager
25	United States	Education	Project manager
26	Canada	Education	Project manager
27	Canada	Education	Mid-management
28	Canada	Consulting	Project manager
29	Australia	Finance	Project manager
30	Canada	Finance	Executive

Exploring Decision Making Effectiveness

Assessing the presence of decision effectiveness requires first establishing a means by which the effectiveness of decisions is assessed. In evaluating effectiveness, I comprehensively assessed the decision making environment described by each participant, and the degree to which there was evidence that the environment (including the participant's involvement within the environment) produced effective decision results. Similarly to other assessments of effectiveness within this study, a scale was used that ranging from 'not effective' through 'somewhat effective' to 'very effective'. The resulting assessment provided a guide by which to evaluate which concepts did ultimately influence decision effectiveness.

VERY EFFECTIVE DECISION ENVIRONMENTS

In order to rate the decision making environment as being 'very effective', there needed to be clear and compelling evidence in the participant reports that the process being described consistently led to good project initiation decisions. Some statements that supported a 'very effective' rating included observations concerning structural components, such as: 'We have specific policy, specific process, and we underscore our process. We have been working on it significantly to make it less bureaucratic. We have streamlined it as appropriate. Looking at value, risk and independence. It is pretty explicit and pretty well followed' (20).

In highly rated environments, the overall process in place was described as being adapted to the context of the organization, with participants expressing high levels of satisfaction that the process was relevant and appropriate. For example, one participant said: 'Following our system will lead you to good decisions' (28). For other participants, effective decisions were a product of their personal influence:

> For me as a sponsor, when I am sponsoring, I expect that the methodology is followed. I will go through it step by step, because I believe I need to lead by example, and because I've been trained in the discipline – I have a level of awareness that many of the other folks don't have. (3)

As well as personal levels of understanding of the process, understanding the culture and politics characterized the ability to influence results successfully; in the words of another participant: 'I have figured out how to work within this culture. It is a relationship-driven organization – if you have the relationship, that is how things get done. Through the back door conversations' (16). Either through structural capabilities or personal influence, a small number of participants were able to demonstrate that they were able to consistently support the production of project initiation decisions, and that the decisions that resulted were effective and appropriate.

SOMEWHAT EFFECTIVE DECISION ENVIRONMENTS

Where I assessed the decision making environment as only 'somewhat effective', the evidence suggested that decision making was inconsistently effective. In these instances, participants indicated that some effective project initiation decisions were produced within the environment they were describing, but that this was not always the case. Sometimes, effectiveness was compromised by political conflicts:

> *If we are getting a negative reaction, we would change the approach. It would start to affect how to determine what kind of schedule was reasonable and what kind of energy required from senior management in order for this to happen – to provide support, to read the riot act, to put resources in. (9)*

Another participant suggested: 'You also have individuals that do the same thing – others higher up in the organizational hierarchy. They can sometimes usurp initiation of other projects that might be a higher priority' (5). Observations about the quality of resulting solutions also reflected solution compromises: 'Ultimately I have to say "We have to do something; we can't do nothing." So initiation is an act of consensus politics, trying to work with all parties to say if it's not 100 per cent, then doing 75 per cent is better than nothing' (22).

The expectations within organizations can also be arbitrary, another participant indicating:

> *You do run into the willy-nilly rules. You ask, 'Why am I doing this?' And the answer is 'Just do it'; or, on other occasions, 'You don't have to do it this time.' A lot of those get driven depending upon who the sponsor is – who is bringing it to the table, how fast they are driving it, if funds are coming from their budget. (25)*

While compromises and challenges exist within these 'somewhat effective' environments, there is evidence that the initiation process does produce results, even where those results are not always optimal.

INEFFECTIVE DECISION ENVIRONMENTS

Where I assessed the decision making environment as 'not effective', there were material disconnects in the participant descriptions which indicated that few decisions occurred effectively within the organizations. These disconnects may be a product of genuinely ineffective capabilities, or may occur between perceived and desired capabilities on the part of participants. The underlying evidence, however, provided strong indications that the decision making environment was inappropriate. Some problems included lack of decision making capacity, one participant indicating: 'We have one or two projects that are adequately resourced. When I say "adequately resourced", they are consuming more than 80 per cent of our human capacity, which means the other 15 projects are really struggling, almost going backwards' (1).

Participants from other organizations mentioned an inherent lack of planning in the context of initiation:

> If we are told to do something, then we proceed to action. We give a wild guess – if it needs to be done in six months, we'll get it done in six months. There is little analysis or research or understanding of what we were told to do in the first place. (2)

Politics was also described as having significant influence in undermining the decision making process: 'Politics are exercised through "You will take on the project." We will be told that this group wants the project to happen; the politics play out, and we are not given any choice in that matter' (26). Politics can result in previous decisions being countermanded; for example:

> Not only can there be a lack of agreement, but there can actually be agreement and we can do the prioritization, and then a week goes by and the same director then says they 'want to revisit that decision'. The result is that it turns the whole thing into a turmoil. (18)

Project initiation decisions can also be described as being almost entirely arbitrary: 'There is no formality. In terms of approval, that would be an executive saying "I want a [project manager] to do this project." From a request perspective, that's how the request would come in' (7). The largest number of participant cases in the study were, for the various reasons described above, identified as having a 'not effective' decision environment.

Framing the Influences on Project Initiation

As mentioned above, there were instances in the study where the influences on project initiation decisions were predominantly personal, and also instances where the influences on initiation decisions were largely determined by the structural environment of the organization. Structural influences were at times process-based, and in other instances more affected by political factors. While the presence or absence of agency was influential in all instances, the manner in which agency was exercised displayed a large degree of variation.

To address the factors that influence decision making effectiveness, it is necessary to establish those instances where project initiation decision making approaches are perceived as being effective, regardless of the constructs and concepts that might be responsible. Then there is a need to define those approaches that are observed to result in decision making success. Finally, we must articulate how those approaches relate to the core category of agency. What will result is an understanding of the major concepts that influence decision making success. These major concepts are illustrated in Figure 3.1.

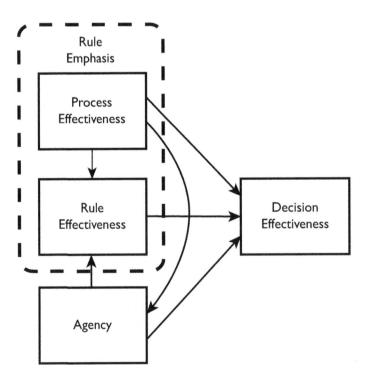

Figure 3.1   Major influences on decision effectiveness

Each of the influences on decision effectiveness illustrated above – process effectiveness, rule effectiveness and agency – are discussed briefly in the following sections, and explored in detail in each of the subsequent chapters. Together, these dimensions comprise the factors that most directly influence decision making effectiveness. Structurally, decision making effectiveness can be shaped by the process environment or the political environment of the organization. The structural dimensions of process and politics also interact with the degree of agency exercised by those in the project shaper role. In political environments, where the implicit rule system has the largest influence, the agency of individuals can augment the political environment of the organization. In process-based environments, where project initiation is determined by formal structures, the independence and agency of those in the project shaper role is actually constrained by the formality and rigour of processes within the organization. Depending upon the environment, the agency of individual actors can also influence decision effectiveness independently.

Structural Influences on Decision Making Effectiveness

An important consideration in understanding the rule system of organizations is whether the emphasis is placed on an explicit or an implicit orientation. As noted above, there were some participants who, in describing structural influences, identified environments that were largely process-driven, while others were described as more political in nature. Where the emphasis is largely process-driven, the rule system is in essence driven by the overall process environment, and is therefore much more explicitly defined. Where the emphasis is largely political, the rule system is driven by the political influences that shape relations in the organization; as a result, the rule system is much more implicit, and the process environment is much less evolved. Understanding the emphasis of the organization, and the degree to which it is implicitly and explicitly focused, is therefore a necessary determinant of rule system orientation. The rule emphasis is not an influence on decision effectiveness, but it is an orienting choice as to which type of rule system is in place.

PROCESS INFLUENCES

The influence of process effectiveness is relevant for those organizations that have an explicit rule emphasis. In these environments, the initiation of projects is associated with adhering to a defined process, in whatever degree of formality exists for that process. The underlying presumption in these contexts is that the more effective the process, the more effective the resulting project initiation decisions are.

For the most part, the relationship of process effectiveness and decision effectiveness is valid. There is a significant and fairly clear, although not exclusive, association between process effectiveness and the resulting decision effectiveness. In general terms, there is a fairly linear relationship between increasing levels of process effectiveness and decision effectiveness.

There are, however, instances where a decision environment is observed to be very effective, even though the process supporting it is viewed as being only somewhat effective or not effective at all. In exploring these specific instances, it becomes clear that the mediating influence on decision effectiveness is not process effectiveness; it is the agency being exercised by the participant outside the process environment. This illustrates why there is no indication in the relationship diagram in Figure 3.1 of agency having a positive influence on process effectiveness; the agency of the participant is not seen to be changing the process or enhancing its effectiveness. Instead, agency is enabling the participant to work outside the process and influence the decision effectiveness directly. The result is that the more effective the process, the more effective the decision, but where ineffective process exists, agency may play a compensatory role.

POLITICAL INFLUENCES

The influence of rule effectiveness is most relevant for those organizations that have an implicit rule emphasis. In these contexts, the rule environment is based upon general understanding, conventions and 'tribal knowledge'. The means by which project initiation is supported is the result of political emphasis more than an understanding of the formalized process. The presumption in these contexts is that the more effective the implicit rule environment of the organization, the more effective the resulting project initiation decisions are.

In those contexts where the rule environment is perceived as not effective, the decision effectiveness is also predominantly seen to be not effective; in those contexts where the rule environment is perceived as being somewhat effective, the decision effectiveness is also predominantly identified as being somewhat effective. There are again some noteworthy exceptions to review. First, there are a few instances where the decision effectiveness in the organization was observed to be very effective, but where the rule effectiveness was not effective; in these situations, the influence of agency is once again the determinant, not the rule system. Second, there were no implicit rule environments where the political influence of the rule system was considered very effective; for the cases observed in this study, the rule environment on its own was at best only somewhat effective, and its corresponding decision effectiveness was also seen as only somewhat effective. The implication is that rule effectiveness within organizations with an implicit emphasis is only part of the influence on decision effectiveness, and agency as an augmenting influence is also required for decision effectiveness to be high.

Individual Influences on Decision Making Effectiveness

The influence of the individual has a varied impact on decision making effectiveness. The individual influences on decision effectiveness are mediated through the exercise of agency. There are instances where individual actions are the sole determinant of decision making effectiveness, and there are also situations where agency exercised by individuals interacts more directly with organizational capabilities. Where agency is seen as contributing to decision effectiveness, it is through participants' perceived flexibility and capacity to act, and their willingness to do so outside or despite the structural elements (the processes or rule systems) that might exist. The exercising of agency may operate independently, or in concert with the rule system of the organization, to influence decision outcomes. It can be exercised in environments with an explicit emphasis as well as organizations that have more of an implicit emphasis. The orientation of implicit versus explicit also has an impact on the manner in which agency is exercised.

Where process dominates the decision making process, comparing agency and decision effectiveness produces what initially appear to be inconsistent results. In several organizations that purported to have a process emphasis, the level of agency indicated a high degree of autonomy and flexibility on the part of the individual actor, and the decision environment was also deemed very effective. At the same time, a number of other organizations' decision environments were rated as very effective where the agency of the participant was perceived as having only limited flexibility, or none at all. This highlights another aspect of the relationship diagram in Figure 3.1: while agency did not have an influence on process effectiveness, there was a constraining relationship between process effectiveness and agency. In those cases where the process effectiveness was seen as being very effective, the perceived agency of the participants was lower, and specifically acknowledged as being less of a focus or emphasis by those participants. The result is that effective process environments appear to have a negative influence on the perception of and need to exercise agency. The overall implication is that agency appears to contribute positively to decision effectiveness in organizations with lower process effectiveness, and is constrained in those contexts with higher process effectiveness.

Comparing agency with decision effectiveness in implicit environments produces a much more demonstrable link between the two concepts than it did in explicit situations where a process emphasis dominated. Here, a clear relationship exists between increasing levels of agency and increasing levels of decision effectiveness. In the study, there were a number of organizations in which the decision environment was seen as not effective, as discussed earlier, even in the face of agency that was characterized as being moderately present. This demonstrates that while agency can be a factor on its own in influencing decision effectiveness, it is not the only factor to have this influence. As in explicit environments, structural influences within the organization can also have a determining influence in decision making effectiveness. The implication is that agency has a positive influence on decision effectiveness, particularly where actors are able to exercise greater levels of autonomy, independence and flexibility; but in instances of moderate agency, organizational factors may still have a greater influence than agency.

Towards a Theory of Project Initiation Decisions

The theory developed within this study articulates the influence of agency and rule emphasis on decision effectiveness. The essential features of the theory are as follows:

- The effectiveness of the project initiation environment is determined by an understanding of decision effectiveness. This is an assessment of the degree to which project initiation decisions are appropriate and reasonable, and in particular the degree to which the environment (including the actions and influences of the participants within that environment) produces consistently effective decision results.

- The degree to which process effectiveness or rule effectiveness might influence decision effectiveness depends on the degree to which the approach to project initiation has an explicit or implicit emphasis, as determined by the rule emphasis within the organization. Where there is an explicit emphasis, the project initiation is guided by an established process, while an implicit emphasis relies upon a rule system composed of collectively understood conventions and informal guidelines.

- Agency has a fundamental influence on decision effectiveness in all contexts. Agency reflects intention, ability and capacity to act – along with a corresponding level of awareness – on the part of individual actors within the rule environment, and their willingness to work within, around or despite the dominant rule system. Agency can work to support the influences of process effectiveness or rule effectiveness, and agency can also override and compensate for organizational inadequacies. Agency can supplement rule effectiveness where required to support effective decisions in implicitly focused environments. While the exercise of agency does not change the process environment, and therefore does not have any direct influence on process effectiveness in explicitly focused environments, it can independently supplement the influences of less effective process environments.

- Where the process environment is particularly effective, the impact of agency can be constrained. The implication is that, because of the emphasis placed on a very formal and consistent process, in the face of a very effective process the action of agency is undesirable. The desire and intent is for project initiation to happen within the context of the process, therefore in these instances the independent actions of actors exercising agency are in fact discouraged.

- Agency is influenced by a combination of structural and personal elements. Those actors who perceive themselves as having high levels of agency view their ability to be successful as a product of their own individual capabilities, while those perceiving themselves as having little agency perceive this to be a product of external constraints. Factors that influence agency are position, decision making involvement within the organization, and the personality of the individual actor.

- Rule effectiveness is influenced primarily by the actions of individuals, where they engage in politically supportive and collaborative behaviours that work to support the rule system in place, and where the detracting influences of negative decision politics and an informal shaper role are not present. While very effective rule systems have not been observed, moderately successful rule systems are able to be augmented effectively through the appropriate exercise of agency by actors. Negative rule systems are the product of inappropriate political behaviours, the presence of obstructive politics and an informal rather than formal project shaper role.

- Process effectiveness is influenced primarily by the formality and consistency of the project initiation process. Process effectiveness is also influenced by the presence of a clear project decision process and the utilization of process-based drivers of influence by actors within the process environment. Very effective process environments have a positive influence on effective decision making, and in these instances the presence of agency is less desirable, and therefore constrained. Process environments that are less successful are able to be augmented and compensated for through actors engaging in the appropriate exercise of agency.

The proposed theoretical framework provides some interesting insights into the various dimensions that are operative, and have an impact, in supporting effective project initiation decisions within organizations:

- Organizations described as having the greatest levels of effectiveness in supporting the initiation of projects within their organizations do so because of either a very formal, very consistent process environment, or the exercise of significant personal levels of agency.

- In organizations where the structural influences of the organization are somewhat effective, individuals performing the project shaper role compensate for this partly through the exercise of agency, and predominantly through the exercise of reinforcing the orientation of the rule system with appropriate influencing behaviours, emphasizing either political or process drivers of influence.

- Where the structural influences of project initiation within organizations are not effective, the presence of agency on the part of individuals playing the project shaper role, or otherwise involved in supporting the decision making process, may make a difference in individual decision situations, but does little to influence the initiation of projects on an on-going basis.

- Where the opportunity may exist for someone to exercise agency in the project shaper role, this can be overridden through unproductive political behaviours or where the project shaper role is not formally recognized.

The focus from the outset of this study has been on how personal influences support and shape the project initiation process. What the results of the study have demonstrated is the presence and impact of these influences, but also that the level of personal influence is dependent upon – and can be enhanced or undermined by – the organizational environment in which individuals find themselves. It is therefore helpful to explore how influence can be reinforced, utilized and also constrained.

Conclusions

While a broad diversity of organizations participated in the research this book is based upon, they have a number of commonalities. In particular, they are trying to get the right projects initiated, and there is a desire to ensure that effective decisions are made as consistently as possible. While effective decisions may be the desired outcome, a broad spectrum of initiation approaches are in place, with wide variation in the actual effectiveness of decisions.

Exploration of the factors that lead to effective decisions reveals that there are organizational factors and individual factors that can jointly contribute to effective decision outcomes. Organizational influences are a product of either the process or the political environment of the organization, but not both. Where there are strong processes in place, while rare, effective decisions are consistently realized as a result of rigorous adherence to a structure that is seen as valued and effective. More politically driven organizations can still realize reasonably effective decisions on a fairly consistent basis where there is a collaborative and constructive political environment, although no organizations consistently realized very effective decisions through political influence alone. Where there is inadequate process, or ineffective or dysfunctional politics, decision making effectiveness is still possible, but this is through the mediation of individuals and the exercise of individual agency.

In some organizations, agency was the only influence that was observed as leading to effective initiation decisions. The willingness of actors to exercise influence, autonomy, independence, and to step out of the organizational rule system when appropriate, was a key influence in ensuring effective project initiation decisions. Agency was also observed as being able to compensate for only moderately effective processes or political environments, thus still enabling effective decisions to be made. In instances where the process was effective, and therefore independent action would be inappropriate or counterproductive, there was also indication that the exercising of agency was constrained.

The subsequent chapters explore these influences in detail. They highlight the circumstances where effective processes are possible, where politics is constructive, and where individuals play a role in ensuring project initiation decisions are made effectively. They also illustrate the consequences of inadequate process and inappropriate politics. Separately, they provide useful insights into each dimension. Together, they reflect the full scope of what was observed in conducting the research.

Chapter 4
When Process Drives Choices

Introduction

As we have already explored, traditional views of decision making presume a rational bias, where all options are formally analyzed and an objective choice is made that maximizes value to the organization. Many organizations purport to make project initiation decisions in just this way. Comparatively few, however, actually do. Making initiation decisions where process drives project choices implies that there is a formalized process that is objectively utilized to evaluate project opportunities, and that it is actually followed. This chapter explores the factors that govern the effectiveness of decision making processes, and in turn the effectiveness of project initiation decisions.

Process effectiveness influences decision effectiveness in those organizations whose rule environment has an explicit orientation, where the process of project initiation is formally defined and articulated. The process defines the rules and expectations of how project initiation is managed, with varying levels of formality and consistency. Some organizations that arguably have an explicit orientation still have very little in the way of process, and correspondingly are perceived as being largely ineffective; at the same time, there are organizations that have processes that are firmly established and are seen as being very effective. The influences on process effectiveness are seen to be those of process formality, process consistency, decision process clarity and the drivers by which personal influence is exercised by participants, as illustrated in Figure 4.1.

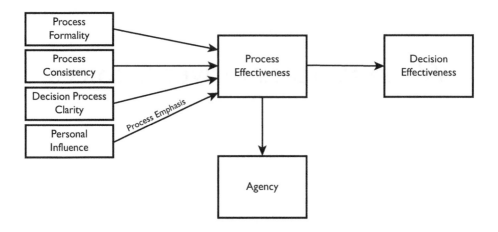

Figure 4.1   Influences on developing process effectiveness

The Value of Formal and Consistent Process

Formality and consistency of initiation processes emerged within the study as two separate concepts that appear to interact and have a strong influence on how projects are actually initiated. Within the study, participants defined a broad range of formality and consistency in the practices by which projects are initiated. Some organizations appear to have virtually no process, and a great deal of inconsistency, while others have an extreme level of formality and consistency in how they assess project opportunities. Within organizations that have explicit rule environments, the processes in place essentially define the rules, establishing the basis of rule emphasis as explicit rather than implicit. There also appears to be a relationship between the degree of formality and consistency of process and the degree of agency that is perceived and exhibited by participants in initiating projects.

In the discussion of formality and consistency by participants, what is described varies considerably. Although 'process formality' and 'process consistency' emerged as two separate concepts in the study, they are strongly related; however, this is not to imply that they vary together in lockstep. Formal processes were not consistently adhered to in participant organizations, and other participants cited consistency in relatively informal processes: 'The process is fairly consistent in terms of how it works, it just isn't formal' (7). There is, however, a fairly strong influence between the formality and consistency of the project initiation process and the relative emphasis (explicit versus implicit) of the rule environment within the organization.

A relatively small number of participants described an initiation process that was very formal and very consistent, and those organizations were far more likely to have an explicitly defined initiation process in place. In this context, the process is rigorously defined and expectation of adherence is high: 'Very. We have tools, processes, and policy. These dictate thresholds, decision making authority and independence' (20). In those organizations described as being very formal and consistent, there also does not appear to be a significant perception that the process is inappropriate or stifling; rather, it is seen as producing value:

> I think our culture has changed to the point that all of our divisional executives buy into the notion that project rigour is required to get anything significant done. If they see it is going to impact their area one way or the other, then they are good at participating. (4)

While the process is adhered to, and agency is constrained as a result, there is a perception that the process as managed is effective and appropriate.

Where there is less formality and consistency in the process, there is a much greater likelihood of the process being perceived as inappropriate or not producing effective results. In discussing lack of formality, participants describe an environment where there are multiple paths to project initiation: 'We have it formally defined, but I would say that more than half of projects initiated in our group don't go the formal route' (1). Lack of formality also appears to be much more likely to result in situations where politics influence the operation of the decision making process: 'Different decisions are made in different ways. We don't have a formal process – sometimes projects are initiated because someone says so. Because they are high enough on the totem pole, now we are doing it' (5).

Lack of consistency in process also results in challenges in managing the project initiation process, as reflected by one participant, who commented: 'Not very. Want to say half and half, but not sure that is right. I think the organization does the best they can in terms of planning, but we don't plan in advance' (13). This approach again results in multiple paths that are available to project initiation: 'A lot of times it is driven by how urgent the initiative has to be implemented, how large it is, what part of the organization is running with it' (21). Lack of formality and lack of consistency in process correlate with a much greater range of approaches by which projects are initiated, as well as lack of clarity in how the process itself works.

Formality and consistency of process are not directly tied to having an explicit rule environment in place. While those organizations whose participants indicated high levels of formality and consistency were more likely to have an explicit rule system, those organizations described as having less formality and consistency may be either explicitly or implicitly focused. Depending upon this focus, the influence of process versus politics is seen to vary, as do the causes of perceived constraint concerning agency. Organizations described as having more implicit rule systems are more likely to have any process that does exist be largely ignored, and the constraints on agency are more likely to be attributed to politics; those organizations described as having more explicit rule systems are more likely to be attempting to reinforce the process, while still being constrained by lack of adherence, but are more likely to view constraints on agency as being a result of process. While the results are the same – constrained agency and flexibility, and frustration with failure to adhere to espoused principles – the underlying drivers leading to constraints and frustration trace back to different sources.

A clear relationship is demonstrated between the level of formality of the process and the perceived effectiveness of the process. Where there is a progressively higher level of process formality, there is also a correspondingly high level of process effectiveness. The implication is that where organizations have an explicit rule emphasis, the level of formality of that process has a direct and positive relationship on process effectiveness.

While there is also a demonstrated relationship between the level of consistency of the process and the perceived effectiveness of the process, it is less definitive than that for process formality. Where the level of process consistency is very high, the process effectiveness is in almost all instances seen as very effective. The organizations where process is described as somewhat effective, all of which evidenced only some formality, actually varied in observed consistency, ranging from low to moderate to high levels. Organizations described as having processes that are not effective are still described as being moderately consistent, even where they vary in formality. The implication is that those organizations that are very consistent also appear to have very effective processes, but that lower levels of effectiveness and formality have more variety in levels of consistency.

Decision Process Clarity

The decision process defines the mechanics behind how the actual decision of whether to proceed with a project or not is made. As in the case of the actual initiation process, a great diversity of practices in the process of decision making were described by participants. In some organizations, the decision process was clear, formal and broadly understood. In other organizations, the process of arriving at decisions was described as arbitrary and unclear. The clarity of the decision process appears to have an influence on the broader process environment, and the degree to which those processes are seen as being effective. Decision process also appears to influence the overall level of agency participants perceive themselves as retaining.

The largest influence described by participants was where there was a lack of clarity or visibility in terms of how the decision making process worked within their organization. Where the process was clear, regardless of whether the decision was made by a board, an executive team or a single executive, participants did not perceive there to be a significant issue or problem. There was typically simple acceptance of the decision making process as it existed and was practised: 'The decision is always the [head of the organization's]. We make recommendations that we think it is a good fit, but ultimately is the [head of the organization's] decision to proceed or not' (8).

An unclear or arbitrary process is perceived as having a much greater level of impact on the decision making process. Not only the process, but also the criteria that must be met in presenting a project for potential project initiation can be misunderstood: 'I'm not sure the basis on which the decision would be made. I would hope it would be made based upon how well the proposed effort would meet with their requirements, but can't be sure' (23). Some participants extend descriptions of this arbitrariness and uncertainty to an open question about what is required for projects to in fact be initiated. One participant, describing the failure to adhere to the defined decision process, said:

> *At the moment, while we put up a quarterly paper with all of the prospective investment opportunities on the table, over the last twelve months we haven't had one of those single projects approved. During the course of the intervening months other decisions have been made that preclude us proceeding with any of the projects that have gone the formal route. (1)*

The consequences described by those participants working with an unclear or arbitrary process were that there was no clarity about how, when or according to what criteria an initiation decision would proceed.

As noted, where organizations were described by participants as having a clear decision making process – regardless of the actual nature and mechanics of that process – the participants did not indicate issues with the process and broadly described acceptance of the process in place; on the other hand, those who described an unclear and arbitrary process reported significant issues in supporting the initiation of individual projects or navigating the overall environment of the organization. The consequence is a process that is seen as being not effective. Participants also indicated that they perceived little flexibility or agency where the decision making process was not effective, which resulted in their perceiving little flexibility or autonomy in being able to compensate or work around the inadequacies that existed in the decision making process.

Having some level of formality in place has an influence on the effectiveness of process. The distinction that needs to be understood is between organizations which are described as having an arbitrary and unclear process of project initiation decision making, and those that have some degree of formality in the decision process. While the actual process, and its level of formality, may vary considerably, the presence of some level of formality was observed in all cases whose processes were identified as being very effective, as well as for many of those whose processes were identified as being somewhat effective. Where there was an arbitrary or unclear decision making process, the process was identified as being not effective or only somewhat effective. The implication is that where the decision making process is arbitrary or unclear, it detracts from overall process effectiveness.

Personal Influence

Related to the idea of agency is how participants see themselves influencing the project initiation and decision making processes in their organizations, and the factors they draw on to exercise influence. In this study, participants were asked to identify how they demonstrated their personal influence and established credibility in supporting the project initiation process. The range of personal drivers by which people establish their influence is not only broad, but it has strong correlations to how they see themselves and the environment in which they operate. There also appears to be a degree to which personal influence has an impact on agency, and how agency is exercised.

The level of diversity in how people perceive themselves influencing the project initiation process is significant because of the impact this self-perception has on how they describe the effectiveness of the process in their organization, and their relative satisfaction with the decision making environment. As discussed above, the decision making environment is strongly shaped by whether there is an explicit or implicit emphasis on decision making, and by the overall formality and the overall consistency of the rule environment. While there should be a correlation between the environment of the organization and the factors that influence and credibility within the organization, the drivers that participants highlight are often much more related to their own personal values than those of the organization.

The drivers that emerged from the interviews can be divided into two major categories: process drivers and political drivers. The process drivers focus on the credibility, knowledge and reputation of the individual. They highlight the degree to which participants emphasize 'diligence', 'experience', 'process' and 'reputation' as means of establishing their credibility in the project initiation process. Process drivers emphasize participants being willing to do the homework, demonstrating the background and having the experience and track record of delivery that show technical and subject knowledge. It is about: 'demonstration of preparation and understanding of the material – and of your subject area. ... Being able to respond to questions and concerns of other members of the panel, that you are responding to. Credibility in being able to address the issues' (4).

Another participant said: 'I am able to establish credibility with them. I can make a technical decision – the one that needs to be made even when they don't like it' (6). The emphasis on process drivers is largely rooted in competence, and the ability to project that competence to the rest of the organization.

What is significant in terms of the personal drivers of influence is that their impact largely appears to be determined by whether implicit or explicit rules are emphasized within the organization. Where participants highlighted that the rule system emphasized explicit rules, there appeared to be greater impact when those same participants then leveraged process-based drivers in exercising personal influence. Where the organization had a rule system that emphasized implicit rules, there appeared to be a greater impact when political drivers were leveraged. When participants identified the drivers they most frequently emphasized in establishing credibility within their roles, however, they seemed to tend to emphasize those drivers that they personally valued and perceived as establishing credibility, rather than those that had the greatest impact within their organization. The misalignment between environment and influence drivers also appears to determine the degree to which participants perceive that they have flexibility and opportunities to make an impact in the project initiation process.

Where there is an emphasis on aspects of influence that reinforce process and experience dimensions, there appears to also be a positive influence on process effectiveness. In those cases where process effectiveness was described as being very effective, more participants identified using drivers of 'diligence', 'experience' and 'reputation' as a means of reinforcing personal influence. Drivers of 'diligence', 'process' and 'experience' were also observed where the decision making process was at least somewhat effective. These drivers of influence were less likely to be observed where the process was seen as not effective. This implies that the more effective the process in organizations with an explicit rule emphasis, the more participants are likely to reinforce this by emphasizing aspects of personal influence that are more process-focused.

Constraining Agency

The degree of agency exercised by participants was a strong theme throughout many of the results of this study. The exception was where there was a robust and highly effective process that defined the initiation process within organizations. In these cases, participants willingly let go of their influence in favour of allowing the process of the organization to drive the initiation of projects. Even where participants were in an executive role with a comparatively high level of positional power and influence, they indicated an expectation and commitment to rigorous process adherence. Rather than attempting to override or influence the outcomes of the process, they allowed the process to work in the manner it was designed. This was the only instance in which organizational capabilities had the effect of constraining the ability and willingness of participants to exercise agency.

The consequences for understanding the interaction between process effectiveness and agency are as follows:

- In instances where there are high levels of process effectiveness, agency is constrained and does not contribute to decision making effectiveness. In these cases, acting autonomously or operating outside the organization's rules is seen as counterproductive and not helpful. Instead, participants work within – and champion – the operation of the process.

- Where there are moderate levels of process effectiveness, agency can have a compensating influence. In these instances, participants are in essence supplementing the effectiveness of the process through the provision of personal support and assistance.

- Where the process is ineffective, the only compensating influence in terms of decision making effectiveness is the exercise of agency. In these circumstances, it is individual autonomy and independent action that ultimately determine the effectiveness of the decisions being made.

Case Study: Process Influences

One participant scenario which demonstrates the influence that strong and effective process can have on decision making effectiveness is drawn from the public sector. The participant was an executive within a Canadian provincial government agency responsible for auditing of government performance and accountability. The projects the organization undertook were typically audit engagements within various government departments, as well as internal corporate projects designed to support on-going productivity improvement and the enhancement of the organization's services.

Within the organization, the rule emphasis was identified by the participant as being mostly implicit, even though there were significant process constraints in place regarding the identification and initiation of projects. In reviewing the description in more detail, it became clear that there was actually a strong explicit focus within the organization, which is why this scenario is included here. The participant observed:

> Sometimes, [I] think it is more important to understand the implicit rules. How does this fit within where the executive is thinking in their strategic planning in the next few years – might not be built into any of the explicit rules. Understanding where the boss wants to go. If you understand that, it helps to understand which projects are likely to go ahead. (8)

In other words, the flexibility lay not in the process that was adhered to in this instance, but the projects that were being proposed and how to shape and position those projects to best meet the needs and direction of the organization.

The process within the organization was very clearly described as very formal and very consistent. There was a well-defined process governing the initiation of projects within this organization, and it was described as being rigorously adhered to, particularly for audit projects:

> Within an audit project, there is so much formality. There needs to be a topic identification, it goes to the operations committee, and we need to determine that it is within the purview of the office. It then goes through planning process to define how will we do it, do we have good criteria, can we do the work? The audit planning memorandum is approved by the challenge committee. We also need to demonstrate that it fits within the mandate of the office. (8)

Speaking of the consistency of their process, the participant said: 'On the audit side, we manage very consistently. Given the standards and peer review that we are subject to, it is very important that we adhere to and follow this process' (8). While corporate projects within the organization were not subject to the same degree of formality and consistency, there was also an effort to introduce more formality to how these projects were initiated.

In establishing personal credibility, the participant identified a combination of process and political drivers. The primary emphasis was on diligence and experience. The participant commented:

> Part of it is what I brought with me when I came here from [previous employer] – years of experience in doing similar work. ... The other part is doing the research to understand what the issues are. It is about spending some time talking to some of the key people, those that could potentially be roadblocks, and understanding and making sure that I've dealt with those concerns. (8)

While the goal was to address roadblocks, part of the approach recognized the need to engage in proactive communications with other individuals within the organization to secure support or eliminate opposition.

The political aspect of project initiation in this scenario appeared to be almost entirely constructive. While the participant was employed within a public sector agency, and the work of the agency could have significant public visibility and speak to the politics of the day, he reported very little in the way of internal politics. Commenting on the politics surrounding a project being considered, the participant said:

It has the buy in that it is something that is appropriate for our office to do. Most of the stuff that I have brought forward, I have not had a problem with any of the executive. The stuff we want to do is seen as having a positive impact on the work that they are doing. (8)

While there might be debate, it was characterized as being constructive in nature: 'Mostly, people are pretty good about being vocal about supporting or not supporting a project' (8). Overall, politics had little overt influence on the project initiation process.

The decision process itself was quite straightforward, and responded to the hierarchical environment within the organization. While the participant was a member of the organization's executive team and had a role in recommending projects for initiation, the decision making process was very clear: 'The decision is always the [head of the organization's]. We make recommendations that we think it is a good fit, but ultimately it is the [head of the organization's] decision to proceed or not' (8). The fact that the direction was ultimately determined by the organization's head was not seen as an issue or a problem; it was stated as a simple fact of how decisions were actually made.

The role of project shaper was one that definitely existed within this organization, particularly for the audit projects the organization conducted. The project shaper's role was to champion the project from the outset, and to provide support throughout the initiation process. In discussing whether the project shaper role existed, the participant's response was:

Oh absolutely. On the audit side, they are called engagement leaders. They are expected to be championing the project, to sell it to the challenge committee. On corporate projects, generally there is also someone put on as project champion in order to discuss it at executive committee. (8)

While the participant was an executive within the organization, and the overall process and rule environment within the organization was seen as quite effective, the perceived agency or flexibility was identified as 'no flexibility'. Because of the formality of the process, the scrutiny to which potential projects were subjected, and the fact that the ultimate decision as to whether a project would proceed was made by the organizational head, the scope and latitude of the participant was quite constrained. He could recommend projects, but those projects would be constrained by the direction of the strategy and the organization. The individual was involved in defining projects, but an extensive and active committee structure had primary responsibility for the actual definition, assessment and formulation of how a project would proceed. What latitude that did exist relied upon learning how the organization worked, then operating within those expectations.

Overall, the scenario described was a very effective project initiation environment, but one driven by the formality and consistency of its process. The rules were perceived as being very effective, and the process was also seen as very effective. There was clarity in terms of how project initiation decisions were made, and also regarding the processes and influences that governed those decisions. The environment was perceived as very collaborative and professional, and the politics as constructive and supportive. However, this was an environment where process and organizational formality dominated and individual agency was constrained. Instead of personal influence or agency in engaging with the project initiation process, there was an expectation of adherence.

Conclusions

In all of the organizations that were characterized by explicit and very effective processes, there was a corresponding constraint on perceived agency by participants. Because of the rigour and formality of process, there was, by the nature of the environment, less room to manoeuvre around the rules within the organization. The value of rigorous consistency was also a constraint on freedom and flexibility. Thus, while all of the participants in this group were comparatively senior within their organizations, they did not perceive a significant level of flexibility or agency. This was not a criticism per se; there was in all instances respect and appreciation for why the formality was in place, but its consequence was a comparative constraint on freedom and latitude of behaviours.

As illustrated in the preceding discussion, several concepts ultimately have an influence on process effectiveness. Process formality and process consistency together have a significant influence, and the formality of the process of project initiation in particular is a determinant of overall process effectiveness. In addition, the degree to which the decision making process itself is not seen as arbitrary or unclear has an influence, and an arbitrary or unclear decision process in turn detracts from overall process effectiveness. In particularly effective process environments, participants are also more likely to emphasize individual influences that reinforce the process focus within the organization. In this study, the dimensions of process formality, process consistency, decision process formality and process drivers of influence were collectively observed to be determinants of process effectiveness.

Chapter 5
When Politics Drives Choices

Introduction

As discussed in the previous chapter, many organizations purport to utilize process in making project initiation decisions, although comparatively few actually do so. The far greater influence on decision making, even where there is the surface appearance of a process capability, is politics. As can be surmised, politics is a far more subjective process of project initiation. It relies upon relationships, power and influence. It is less consistent and more volatile. Where political factors are the primary influences on project initiation decisions, different factors are at play than when decisions rely upon a process. Despite the means of initiation being less formalized and structured, however, political decision making approaches can lead to effective project initiation decisions. This chapter explores the factors that govern the effectiveness of decisions in a politically oriented model, and the subsequent influence on decision making effectiveness.

The rule system in politically oriented environments influences decision effectiveness in those organizations that have an implicit orientation. Although in these situations the rules are more socialized or collectively understood through 'tribal knowledge' rather than being written down, they none the less define the expectations and conventions of how project initiation is conducted within the organization. Some organizations with an implicit emphasis are seen as having rule systems that are 'not effective', while in others the rule system is seen as being 'somewhat effective'. The influences on rule effectiveness are seen to be the drivers of personal influence, decision politics and the formality of the role of the project shaper, as illustrated in Figure 5.1.

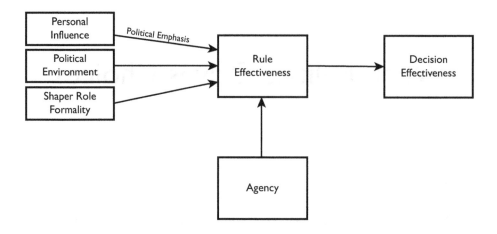

Figure 5.1   Influences on developing rule effectiveness

Personal Influences

The impact of drivers of personal influence has already been discussed in the context of process effectiveness. The second area of emphasis in terms of drivers of personal influence is their impact on rule effectiveness. Where there is a primary emphasis on rule effectiveness, the drivers that are seen to have influence are those that are more political in nature. These reinforce communication, relationships and political engagement within the organization. Their presence indicates the degree to which participants have identified influence to be a product of 'political savvy', 'relationship' and 'proactive communication'. Political influences can also be a product of formal power and influence within the organization, whether that power is a product of position or is delegated. Political drivers reinforce scenarios where relationships are leveraged; for example, one participant said:

> *I have a pretty broad network across the campus – I am able to leverage off those relationships, I am known – good or bad. I may not know who to call, but you know someone who you can call who will know. You can get someone to make introductions for you. (25)*

These drivers reinforce the ability to guide and facilitate agreement, as illustrated by one participant who reflected on the need to:

> *define where we need to go, [and] facilitate getting there in a way that is not about forcing the issue. Start by laying out overall objectives, and*

engage the team in a discussion about action items – what needs to be done to get there. Empower them to go and do that. (13)

In terms of power and position, political drivers enable participants to engage in the power afforded by position and authority: 'The people that tend to be selected are at the right level to do the job. You go in with implicit authority and power' (4). The political drivers are rooted in relationships and power, and the ability to exercise both informal and formal networks within the organization.

Where there is an emphasis on drivers of influence that reinforce political dimensions, there appears to be a positive influence on rule effectiveness. Strategies of 'political savvy', 'proactive communications' and 'relationship' were employed by almost all participants where the rule environment was described as being somewhat effective. Where the rule environment was indicated as being not effective, proactive communications and relationships were identified by comparatively much fewer participants as a strategy for establishing credibility. For those in an environment described as not effective, there was also more of an emphasis of relying on delegation – in other words, of leveraging the power and authority of others – rather than employing one's own strategies. The implication is that the more effective the rule environment is in organizations with an implicit emphasis on political rules, the more participants are likely to reinforce the rule environment with drivers of personal influence that emphasize political dimensions.

Political Environment

The politics underlying the project initiation process contributes significantly to rule effectiveness. Participants described different degrees of political influence on the decision making processes, from a highly interventionist environment to one where political influence was seemingly non-existent. The political environment was described by some as being very constructive and co-operative, while others described an environment that was very hostile, obstructive and unproductive. Clearly, the political environment influences how individual decisions are made. There also appears to be evidence that political considerations influence the process environment within the organization, including the degree to which establishing a process emphasis is possible, and the resulting agency that participants perceive themselves as having in the project initiation process. These influences are explored in more detail below.

As with the other dimensions discussed thus far, a wide range of political practices were described by participants. While a number of them reported that political activity had a strong influence, this was not uniformly the case. In addition, there were two dominant narratives that framed the political behaviour within organizations: constructive and obstructive.

The presence of constructive political behaviours was for the most captured in participant descriptions associated with such terms as 'constructive' and 'buy-in'. In these scenarios, participants indicated the presence of politics that supported and enhanced discussion and decision making within the project initiation process. Participants reflected on situations where disagreements and uncertainty were worked through in a productive fashion; for example, one participant reported: 'I think there is an obligation to address ambiguity quickly – to pursue conversations and share information with the entire steering group. If there tends to be lack of clarity – then probably five other are people also uncertain' (5).

While there were political interactions, they were seen as being necessary in order to define the project successfully:

> Politics at the level I mostly work on is in terms of the competing needs of various groups, and how well the project is going to meet those various needs. That's intrinsic – that's the problem. When I am doing a project I can do it to help this space, or that space. This becomes a critical conversation – too comprehensive, and the project becomes too big; too small, and it doesn't get done. (6)

Another participant expanded on the essential role of politics in supporting the project initiation process:

> I do an awful lot of walking around and confirming things with people, and making sure that I have ticked all the boxes. I have to be quite methodical in terms of the way I approach everything here, just because I know who the personalities are, who actually understands what it is, and who is just making noise. (29)

Constructive political behaviours were not seen as negative, but as the necessary vehicle by which questions were addressed and conflicting expectations resolved.

The presence of obstructive political behaviours was primarily captured in participant descriptions associated with such terms as 'avoidance' and 'disagreement'. They characterized scenarios where politics was seen as negative, and to undermine the process of decision making in the context of project initiation. Speaking of the ability to address conflict, one participant indicated:

> *[The organization] as a culture lets people act out in the room. Everyone lets uncomfortable situation happen, and will pull aside the person later. [The organization] is mostly a risk-averse culture – it doesn't deal with outright confrontation. We will sheepishly address them. And they will do it again next time. (15)*

Avoidance behaviour was characteristic of a number of participant descriptions:

> *Half of executives [are] very supportive of the project, and the others are questioning whether we are at the right level of investment. I don't think anyone is questioning whether it was the right investment, but we are now investing 50–60 per cent more than intended. There are a number of executives who are questioning behind closed doors whether that is an appropriate level of investment. They won't question it in an open forum, though. (1)*

This contrasts sharply with how unacceptable political behaviour was viewed in other organizations: 'If you don't like it, then find another company. Tell them what you think. If they say, "We're doing it anyway," then you have a choice, and the choice is not to stay within the company and sabotage it' (30).

In part, the political difficulties were a product of the organizational environment, as described by one participant in an academic environment, who indicated: 'The interesting thing around universities is that you have this concept of tenure. Faculty with tenure [have] little motivation to compromise – they are trained to critique, to debate, to defend their point of view. There is no incentive to move off a position' (22).

In the context of these organizations, politics was seen not as being constructive, but as a barrier; depending upon the perspective, it was a means of avoidance, of obstruction or of advancing personal interests at the expense of the larger interests of the organization.

What is particularly important regarding the influence of politics is how they affect the other aspects of the project initiation process, and particularly the degree to which participants perceive the process as being effective or not. In particular, where constructive political behaviours were described, there tended to be a great deal more perception of influence on the process, as indicated by the perceived flexibility or agency of the participant. Where obstructive politics predominated, this was seen as a constraint on the exercising of flexibility and agency. The consequence is that those that perceive themselves as having agency are more inclined to describe a positive political environment, while those perceiving little agency or flexibility are more likely to attribute it to the influence of negative political behaviours.

Where there are negative decision politics within the organization, there is a tendency for the rule effectiveness within the organization to be less. The relationship between politics and rule effectiveness is not, for the most part, a positive influence. The presence of decision politics characterized as being 'constructive' was both rare and undifferentiated in its influence on the effectiveness of the rule system. Where the rule effectiveness of the organization was identified as being not effective, however, there was a much greater likelihood of the political influence on decisions being described as 'neutral' or particularly 'negative'. The implication is that decision politics have an inverse influence on rule effectiveness; the more negative the political influence on project initiation decision making, the more likely it is that the rule system is seen as ineffective.

Shaper Role Formality

The role of project shaper was broadly described by participants in the study. While all participants reported that the role of project shaper existed to some degree, for many the role was very informal and not consistent from project to project. Some identified a very formal role that they equated from the outset with the role of project sponsor. Arguably, every participant involved in the study to some degree themselves manifested and embodied the project shaper role, and their responses indicated their own influence on how they shaped potential project opportunities. There also appeared to be an influence between the perceived formality of the project shaper role and the degree of agency participants perceived themselves as being able to exercise.

While all participants reported that the role of project shaper existed to some degree in their organizations, how the role was enacted varied. Some participants clearly identified this role as being that of the sponsor. For example one participant said: 'I don't think it is a role, I think it is an expectation. We understand this is an important part of any organization – we need someone in high enough position, to provide support of the overall project' (5). Other participants identified the role as that of a subject matter expert, or a project manager: 'Most often, and I am only going to deal with the large projects, they are assigned to it because they have a leadership role within the organization. They have some level of expertise within the area the project is dealing with' (3).

In all instances, there was someone who was identified as supporting the project through the initiation process, and relative acceptance of that role.

However, a number of participants reported that the project shaper role was at best informal within their organization. In these instances, a greater number of challenges were observed in securing support and steering projects through the project initiation process. In some instances, the role of project shaper was less concerned with supporting the business than the technology or project management office within the organization. One individual, speaking about whether a project shaper existed, indicated: 'No. Typically not. It is not there formally, but it might be informal. It is more looking at it on the technology side, less business analysis' (26). Another participant reinforced this idea by saying: 'It is a typical role, but not an official one. Technically its supposed to be the executive champion or business sponsor' (6). Where someone is informally assuming the project shaper role, there appears to be lack of support and championing of the project in the organization. The project does not necessarily get the visibility, the support, the attention or the resources it requires in order to be successful: 'A lot of it depends upon the project. It depends on the individual – whether that person is respected in the organization. This is a very political organization. And it depends upon how it is going to impact their own organization' (7). Projects in organizations that have an informal shaper role appear to struggle more to get support for initiation than those with a formal role. This again has an impact on the perceived flexibility and agency of the participant to work within and across the organization.

Where there is an informal project shaper role, there is a tendency for the rule system to be less effective. In all of those organizations where the rule effectiveness was identified as being at least 'somewhat effective', the role of the project shaper was identified as being 'formal'. In all the instances where the project shaper role was described as being 'informal', the rule effectiveness was identified as being 'not effective'. While rule shaper formality does not necessarily ensure effectiveness of the rule system, lack of formality appears to have a negative influence. The implication would appear to be that where the project shaper role is informal, there is a greater likelihood that the rule system will be identified as being ineffective.

Support of Agency

In political environments, agency was observed to have a much greater and more direct influence on decision making effectiveness. In fact, political environments appear to require the exercise of agency if effective decisions are to be made. No organization with an implicit emphasis was described as having a very effective decision making process, except where the participants also exercised strong levels of agency. In fact, organizations whose project initiation process is more political in nature are much more likely to have an ineffective decision making process.

Personal factors play a strong role overall in promoting effective decision making in political environments. In addition to the influence of agency, effective decision making in these contexts is supported by emphasizing credibility through political influences and ensuring that the project shaper role is formally defined. All of these are factors that are attributable to – and in the control of – individuals in support of the decision making process. The only organizational factor that has an influence is the nature of the political environment; in the absence of constructive politics within the organization, there appears to be very low effectiveness in making project initiation decisions.

Case Study: Political Influences

The following scenario which illustrates project initiation decision making in the presence of constructive politics is also drawn from the public sector. The organization in question was a department within a large North American municipality. The participant was a director of the organization, responsible for the construction of large-scale transportation infrastructure projects.

The rule emphasis within the organization was identified as being strongly implicit. In discussing which types of rules it was more important to focus on, the participant responded: 'Understand the implied ones – explicit ones you can read, the others you have to get off the wind. They are more difficult. They are the more challenging things to tackle' (9). The implication is that while explicit rules can and do exist, they are much more straightforward and easily engaged with than implicit rules; the latter are more ethereal, but also much more critical to understand and engage with.

The process in place within this organization had some formality. Historically, the formal process had little emphasis within the organization.

There was currently an initiative under way, led from the top of the organization, to change this. Discussing the current process environment, the participant said: 'It hasn't been as formally defined as it is going to be .... The rigour around that is going to improve. There will be much more expectation regarding some of those first steps: initiation, rationale, support for benefits' (9). In terms of consistency, the process was seen as very inconsistent: 'Right now very inconsistent. Part of the rationale for improving' (9). The consequence of both the relative informality and the high level of inconsistency was that the project initiation process was currently viewed as being fairly ineffective.

In working to support the initiation process, the participant reinforced both process and political dimensions of influence. It was presumed that the participant needed a baseline of credibility. In discussing what shaped personal influence, the participant said: 'I think partly by performance. If we can show that we do things well, then we can start talking about the things that we do well. The underpinning thing. You build credibility by doing things well' (9). While credibility was a necessary underpinning, however, the primary emphasis discussed by the participant was more politically motivated, stating that there was a need to focus on relationships, proactive communications and political savvy. The participant highlighted the success of 'those that have been able to understand the political winds' (9), as well as the importance of building effective relationships: 'Another thing is I make sure that I take the opportunity to engage in the other directors in social opportunities – develop personal relationships. Get the ability to pick up the phone and get support and assistance' (9). The implication is that while credibility is a presumed baseline, there is a strong need to establish and maintain effective political networks, and to engage other members of the organization constructively in supporting the project initiation process effectively.

Politics in this organization had a strong influence. This is perhaps not entirely surprising, given that it was a municipality in the public sector, therefore politics was an inevitable part of the environment. However, the political environment strongly emphasized the need to engage in consultation and to seek buy-in for decisions. In discussing political influence, the participant said: 'Try and see what kind of general support, or general opposition, there would be. If we are going into business units and getting support, then OK. If we are getting negative reaction, then we would change our approach' (9). Ensuring political support was critical: 'No point in going if you don't think you can garner big-P and little-p political support' (9). A significant part of the project initiation process therefore emphasized consultation and securing buy-in from critical stakeholders, and shaping what would be proposed based upon what those stakeholders were prepared to support.

The decision making process in the organization involved a recommendation by the senior administrative team within the organization, and an approval vote by Council. Officially, administration was responsible for focusing on the technical aspects of the project, while the focus of Council was on the political considerations: 'in practice, there are a lot of political considerations in our projects' (9). Even for large projects, the focus in the decision making forum was very high-level:

> *Would do probably a presentation on some of the major thoughts, direction, ideas. No more than five slides. A five-to-seven minute presentation and let them ask questions. Outline and get their agreement on the approach that they would support …. But that would be about all the time you are going to get. Need to be very succinct. (9)*

Once a project was presented for consideration, there was a presumption that consultation and technical assessment had occurred. What was actually debated in making the decision, however, was comparatively brief and high-level.

In this organization, the participant reported that the role of project shaper existed, and would typically be performed by a subject-matter expert. In discussing the shaper role, the participant said: 'What happens in something like this is that the general manager would appoint someone within their group to do that. Had some things in [one business area] – an individual was appointed at a mid-management level to carry that forward' (9).

Much of the credibility of the project shaper role was highly dependent upon support within the organization:

> *If there is an initiative that has organizational support, then you would see a lot of people coming behind that. If it is being imposed, then they might be quite isolated. A lot of it has to do with support, and the project itself. And the support for the project. (9)*

While the shaper role existed, it was critically dependent upon political support for the project, and the degree to which the project itself was seen as being valued.

The participant observed that he had some flexibility in terms of perceived agency within the organization. The organization was highly political in its internal operations, and required support and buy-in from those who were impacted by a project in order for it proceed. In discussing the ability to exercise influence, the participant said:

> *Probably more than half of the challenge is the need to know the rules – where to step and where not to step. Where you can count on performance and not performance. If those guys never fulfil, then the initiative will drop with no backup. You need an understanding of where there is support, and where that will actually result in performance. (9)*

While there was some flexibility by the participant to influence the process, much more influence was exercised by others. Playing within the rules that are socially sanctioned by the organization is critical to overall success.

In this scenario, there were deficiencies in the project initiation process and challenges in how decisions were made about project opportunities. While there was an initiative under way to improve the formality and consistency of the process, it was an open question whether or not that would have traction given the amount of political influence that drove how the project initiation process actually operated. In this instance, influence in project initiation was a combination of having some agency, along with a recognition of the need to work within the rules. That requires an understanding of the rule environment, which is driven by politics, relationships and influence.

Conclusions

The characteristics that are common in these examples encompass both organizational and personal dimensions. While all organizations that were identified as having an implicit emphasis highlighted the influence of politics, organizations in this instance were identified as having a predominant emphasis on constructive politics. In addition, participants in the project shaper role made a significant contribution to the overall effectiveness of the project initiation process. Those participants in the project shaper role identified themselves as having at least some agency. In addition, they reinforced the political drivers of influence, namely political savvy, proactive communications and relationships. Also emphasized to a lesser extent were position and delegation, reinforcing influences of positional power and authority as well. Rule environments that were characterized as being somewhat effective drew on constructive political behaviours within the organization, as well as these behaviours being reinforced and exemplified by those individuals playing a project shaper role.

As illustrated in the preceding discussion, several concepts have an influence on rule effectiveness. While there were no organizations with a very effective rule system in this study, differences were observed between ineffective and somewhat effective rule systems. Drivers of personal influence that emphasized political characteristics were evident in circumstances where rule systems were seen as at least somewhat effective. The presence of greater levels of agency was also perceived by participants as augmenting the effectiveness of the rule system. Where there were ineffective rule systems, the decision politics was more likely to be perceived as negative and dysfunctional. In addition, where the project shaper role was perceived as informal, the rule system was more likely to be perceived as ineffective. Collectively, within this study the dimensions of political drivers of influence, decision politics, formality of the project shaper role and the presence of agency were observed to be primary determinants of rule effectiveness.

Chapter 6
When Individuals Drive Choices

Introduction

In conducting this research, one of the key challenges was initially identifying a core category of analysis that explained what was being observed across all of the participant experiences. Identifying a core concept was complicated and difficult, given the broad range of descriptions and scenarios that were described by participants. There were structural themes that emerged, of politics, process and formality, that all in some way appeared to be relevant to understanding the cases. The role of participants and their influence also clearly had an impact on an initiation in some cases, but not in all. There were instances where the influence on decision making was predominantly personal; there were also instances where the influence was predominantly structural, and those structural influences were themselves sometimes process-based and in other instances driven politically. What ultimately emerged, after a considerable period of reflection and analysis, was the concept of agency.

Recognizing the influence of agency was complicated by the way in which it was manifested in different contexts. In heavily process-oriented environments, agency was constrained; it was identified as actively being limited based upon the perceived need within the organization to adopt a formal and consistent approach to project initiation. In politically oriented environments, agency could enhance or compensate for organizational inadequacies or lack of clarity. In other contexts, agency was the sole means by which decisions were actually influenced. While the influence of agency varied, however, awareness of it as a concept – and the degree to which it was utilized or constrained – was constantly present. Agency became the critical concept that weaved through all of the participant descriptions in some manner and form.

In the context of this study, the definition of agency that is being utilized is that proposed by Dietz & Burns (1992) in their discussion of the freedom of choice and range of options that actors have when it comes to engaging with social rules. They suggest that: 'The rules known by an actor influence their behaviour in a given situation. But this realization of rules into practice cannot be mechanical. Rules must be interpreted to be used in a particular context' (Dietz & Burns, 1992, p. 189). In other words, actors have a range of options when faced with a decision situation, and in exercising agency, will interpret the context and the rules they perceive as being relevant in choosing how they will respond. In exercising agency, they have freedom and flexibility to respond within or work around the rules that are perceived or professed to exist. While the phenomenon described as 'agency' by Dietz & Burns was mentioned by some of the participants when they were discussing how projects were initiated within their organizations, it was not universally present. The implication is that agency does not always exist or is not always perceived to be available – or at least available fully – to participants, and an understanding of how agency manifests or wanes is important when considering how the perceived rules of project initiation are actually interpreted.

Given its relatively significant influence on the process of project initiation, it is important to explore the drivers and factors that support the creation – or inhibit the exercising – of agency. While the previous sections discussed the influences of different degrees of agency, what is now necessary is the integration of these perspectives into a single view of the overall influences by which agency is shaped. The insights gained within this study indicate that the embodiment of agency is in large part a product of power. The cases in this study show that considerable flexibility is a result of a combination of influences that include position, role, expertise and influence. Agency also appears to be a product of personality. The primary influences of agency are illustrated in Figure 6.1.

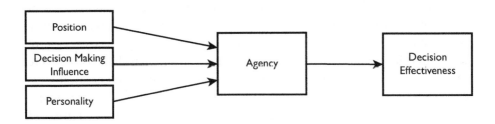

Figure 6.1   Influences on the development of agency

Characterizing the Influence of Individuals

Within the findings of the study, agency is a fully developed construct. Participants described situations where it existed strongly, where it partially existed, and where it did not exist at all. Some participants said that they had considerable latitude to work across the organization, around the rules and outside the constraints of processes. Other participants indicated that they had some latitude and freedom of choice or expression, but only within narrowly defined or constrained contexts. Finally, several participants described an environment where they felt entirely constrained by the processes and rule systems imposed by their organizations, with little to no latitude for choice or movement. Not only was the described degree of agency very broad, its implications for project initiation decisions and decision participation are quite significant. To appreciate this significance, it is important to explore more fully how agency is manifested within the project initiation process.

CONSIDERABLE FLEXIBILITY

Where participants described having considerable flexibility, or agency, they identified three primary drivers. Participants indicated considerable flexibility within the rule system in situations where they actively influenced the definition of rules, where they were willing to work around the rules, or where they had developed a deep understanding of the organizational culture.

Two participants were in fact responsible for the development of the rules regarding project initiation in their organizations, and therefore also felt that there was considerable latitude to influence, change or at times subvert those rules. For example, one participant indicated:

> *The pitfall is I understand the rules in my own head, but sometimes they don't get conveyed. Sometimes the problem is that the rules are my rules, and they haven't been formally adopted within the organization or in the PMO – part of the vision that I have that hasn't really made its way out yet. (3)*

Those with high levels of agency were also willing to bypass the rules that they imposed on others: 'We want to create some working proofs to bring staff up to speed, but don't want to go through the formal approval process – because I don't think it's necessary' (17). The strong implication that emerged from both examples was that because they strongly influenced the rules, these participants also had a great deal of flexibility in how they responded to the rules.

The second primary driver of considerable agency was a fundamental and stated willingness to work around the rules. In the view of one participant:

> *My projects seldom fail. I can usually take the approach that I believe needs to occur to get traction. It often takes a long time to get the initial traction. But I understand how to work with the culture of most of the sites – by nature that is where I started. (6)*

This individual's willingness to work around the rules was reinforced by a strong level of perceived autonomy: 'I am seen as an iconoclast. It is why they keep me around, but they are also careful how they use me' (6). The implication is that not only was the participant willing to work around the rules, there was a tacit expectation on the part of the organizational executive team that this is exactly what would happen.

The final primary driver of where participants indicated having considerable agency was as a product of having a strong understanding of the culture, and of how to operate effectively within it. Two participants in the study indicated that they had a very strong understanding of the organizational culture and what it took to get projects initiated. In the words of one participant: 'I have adapted and learned along the way. Experience and trial and error. Now that I have a level of credibility, what used to take more effort now takes less' (10). This observation was echoed by a second participant, who indicated: 'I have figured out how to work within this culture. It is a relationship driven organization – if you have the relationship, that is how things get done. Through the back door conversations' (16). In this context, relationships, politics and credibility were what enabled initiation decisions to get made, and developing these was key to establishing flexibility.

In all of the above instances, the qualities that underlie the attainment of considerable flexibility are personal ones. The participants who indicated a strong level of agency in decision making firmly believed that they had it, and were confident in their ability to make decisions, engage in political negotiations and successfully influence the process of project initiation. The implication was that independent of many of the other conditions that existed within their organizations, the individuals with the most flexibility had the personal influence necessary to be successful.

SOME FLEXIBILITY

Those who had some flexibility or agency described decision making environments where they faced limitations on their ability to influence the project initiation process. Unlike those who indicated that they had considerable flexibility, a much larger number of participants indicated having only some flexibility. For these participants, there appeared to be two primary forms of constraint: process and politics.

Where there are perceived constraints through process, it is expected that some level of process will be adhered to. Because some processes are defined, or there are formal expectations regarding some aspects of the project initiation process, these are seen as constraints on the flexibility of individual participants involved in the project initiation process. Speaking of the organization's rule environment, one participant commented:

> Have to follow the explicit ones, but here there are way more implicit ones. Emphasis gets on implicit, because there [are] more of them. If I have to bend one or the other, the bias is towards implicit ones. But there are some explicit ones that you know you cannot compromise. Sometimes those are ones that are just de facto requirement. If you don't do those, you won't get anywhere. (19)

Another participant offered: 'Would have to say the explicit, and the only reason I make the distinction is because those have legal ramifications, policy issues. Knowing they are stated for a specific reason, to cover you and the institution' (25). In addition, some process-based environments indicate consequences for the individual for violating the process:

> Our process is quite consistent, because culturally we recognized that for it to work we have to be fairly tough. If someone has not filled this out, it hasn't gone through the steps, they have no support from the company to proceed with what they want. If what they are dealing with has a level of urgency, then they have a really harsh conversation and they get what they want, but it is something that hurts their career slightly. (30)

Among these participants, while there was still a recognition of latitude within the rule system governing project initiation, there was a view that actions were constrained within the defined and explicit rules, at least with respect to what they encompassed.

The second influence on the limits to participants' agency was a recognition that there were others within the organization who had political influence over the decision. In other words, the participants did not have exclusive autonomy over the initiation process and were subject to both the decisions and also the desires and agendas of other organizational stakeholders. As one participant observed: 'In this environment, I can't get into anything but trouble by initiating something on my own, without consensus and agreement of my colleagues' (22). With regard to the influence of politics in the organization, another participant observed: 'There is the informal route where you simply lobby the executive and get the approval. You need to go to the more powerful executive if you want that to proceed' (1). In this context, political support at another level of the organization was required in order for the project initiation process to proceed.

While participants were still able to exercise some influence and agency, in the above illustrations it was seen to operate within established constraints, whether those constraints were process-based or political. In these situations, there is not an unconstrained level of autonomy, but instead participants need to work within the bounds of their organizations, even though there is some latitude for movement within the bounds themselves. The participants indicating that they had 'some flexibility' formed a sizeable group, consisting of 17 responses. These participants were also located at varying levels within their organizational hierarchies, from project manager through mid-management to executive, indicating that agency is not simply a product of position within the organization. The majority of participants mentioned having less agency than they would have desired, or than might have been implied by their positions. The ability to exercise agency was therefore not directly tied to the position or level of seniority held in the organization.

NO FLEXIBILITY

While most of the participants indicated that they had some flexibility – and therefore agency – within the project initiation process in their organizations, some participants reported no flexibility in how the initiation process was conducted. There were two primary influences underlying this situation: the rigidity of process and the predominance of politics.

In these situations, unlike those where participants had some agency, the process was so rigid that participants did not see any room for manoeuvring or flexibility. The rules were seen as being 'the rules', and participants as a result perceived themselves as having no range of movement within the organization.

In one case, there was a genuinely high degree of rigour, formality and scrutiny within the organization regarding the initiation of individual projects. The organizational process set out very explicit requirements for how initiation was to be managed, and how opportunities were to be evaluated and challenged. Despite the fact that the participant was a member of the executive team, the organization was sufficiently hierarchical and procedural in its operation that the participant perceived little latitude: 'There are very explicit rules on how projects should be initiated' (8). Other participants were more junior in their organizations, and they perceived that the process formally defined and articulated what was required in order for a project to be initiated, and that these guidelines were rigorously adhered to. These participants conveyed no sense or indication that politics was an influence governing these decisions. One participant observed: 'The rules would be very strict, and we would be forced to adhere to them. On a project like this, they would not ever not be adhered to' (21).

The second influence on having no flexibility is the impact of politics within the organization. In this context, a lack of flexibility arises when the political influence within the organization is seen as being sufficiently strong that participants have no latitude for discretion or agency with respect to their involvement in the project initiation process. One participant, despite being an executive, perceived the organization as so hierarchical and political that the individual had both little influence in the process and a strong need to support and serve others who did have political influence: 'Can be extremely challenging. As administration, I'm a second class citizen' (22). Of two other participants, one was lower in the organizational structure, and the other was working in the capacity of a consultant outside of the formal organization chart. Both saw politics as influencing the initiation of projects, and both had a high level of resentment regarding the existence of politics. Because of the political influence, the rules were not seen as clear and were perceived to be in constant flux. Speaking of the political constraints, one of the participants observed: 'We will be told that this group wants the project to happen. The politics play out, and we are not given any choice in that matter' (26). Because of the strength of the political environment, the ability to exercise agency was seen as non-existent.

While a total lack of flexibility was identified as a reality by a much smaller number of participants than those who had some or considerable flexibility, it was still a significant group within the findings. Moreover, it was not strictly a product of position within the organization – two of the six participants who indicated that they had no flexibility also identified themselves as executives within their organizations, which in most contexts would imply possessing a great deal more autonomy and agency than they actually perceive themselves as having. These findings also highlight that agency can be constrained by the operation of both process and politics.

IMPLICATIONS OF AGENCY

With regard to agency, it was interesting to note that in the descriptions of the different dimensions discussed in the previous section, participants who indicated considerable flexibility credited their ability to exercise agency to factors that largely drew upon their internal belief in their own influence and abilities. Those who indicated that they had no flexibility primarily ascribed the lack of agency to external forces. Those who identified themselves as having some flexibility indicated aspects that were both personally influenced and externally constrained. This suggests that agency is in part internally motivated, and also that it can be externally constrained. Given its influence on the project initiation process as observed by participants, understanding the sources of agency and how it is developed is worth exploring in more detail. The following section expands on the relevant insights that have emerged from this study.

Influence of Position

One of the influences on agency appears to be that of position. While there is not a strict correlation, there is sufficient indication in the study findings to suggest that a relationship exists. Those participants who indicated considerable levels of agency tended to be at an executive or mid-management level, those with only some flexibility tended to be at a mid-management or project manager level, and those with no flexibility tended to be exclusively at the project manager level. As noted above, this does not comprise a strict correlation: one executive indicated having only some flexibility, and two indicated that they had no flexibility. As has been noted earlier, these constraints on agency are a product of the political and process environment within the respective organizations, where the individuals do not have – or do not perceive that they have – an ability to influence, work around or adapt the rules. The presence or absence of agency was not necessarily identified as being problematic in these instances; it was not necessarily indicated as being desirable by the participants that they should have a greater level of agency at this level. The overall results, however, do suggest that the higher in an organization someone rises, the greater the level of agency they will tend to possess.

Decision Making Influence

There is also an impact from decision making influence on the promotion of agency. In particular, there appears to be a correlation between the level of involvement in the decision making process regarding project initiation decisions and the level of agency that participants have and are able to exercise.

There was a relationship between decision involvement and perceived agency, particularly for those participants who perceived that they had moderate or high levels of agency. Those who had considerable flexibility either participated in decisions or had input into decisions. Those with some flexibility typically either had input into decisions or made recommendations. Those with no flexibility had no input into decisions or had no decision influence, although one participant indicated participation in the decision, but felt that they had no flexibility in terms of agency within the project initiation process. Also, one participant with no flexibility made recommendations in the context of the project initiation process. Overall, however, it appeared that the greater the level of agency within the organization, the greater the amount of involvement participants had in the decision making process regarding project initiation.

Influence of Personality

As has been noted above, those with the greatest amount of agency in the project initiation process in their organizations were those who perceived themselves as having a considerable amount of personal influence. Interestingly, this appears to also be in part a product of the personal characteristics and underlying preferences of the individual. While this is predominantly a qualitative study, one quantitative component that was inserted into the design was an assessment of personality preferences based upon Jung's theory of psychological types. The Insights Discovery assessment instrument produces numerical results on a six-point scale indicating the relevant preferences that correspond largely to each of the core combinations of attitudinal and rational functions. These are constructed predominantly by combining each of the attitudes of extroversion and introversion with each of the rational functions of thinking and feeling. The relationship of attitudes and functions within the Insights Discovery model is illustrated in Figure 6.2.

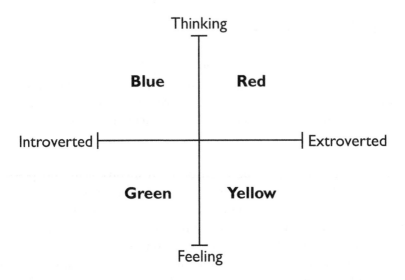

Figure 6.2   Insights Discovery personality assessment dimensions

COMPARING AGENCY AND PERSONALITY

Comparing the perceived categories of agency with the means of the Insights Discovery scores of the associated participants resulted in observed levels of variation within each level of perceived agency, as well as within each of the Insights Discovery preferences. Table 6.1 illustrates the mean Insights Discovery colour scores at each level of agency observed within the study.

Table 6.1   Rule agency versus mean Insights Discovery score

	Blue	Green	Yellow	Red
No flexibility	4.99	3.61	2.15	2.82
Some flexibility	3.79	3.79	3.04	2.95
Considerable flexibility	3.39	2.04	3.18	4.46

As can be observed in Table 6.1, there was a material difference in scores at each level of agency:

- Those who had a higher score for 'Insights blue' (predominantly extroverted and thinking) were much more likely to indicate that they perceived 'no flexibility', and far less likely to indicate that they perceived 'some flexibility' or 'considerable flexibility'.

- Those who had a higher score for 'Insights green' were more likely to indicate that they perceived 'no flexibility' or 'some flexibility', and were much less likely to indicate that they perceived 'considerable flexibility'.

- Those who had a higher score for 'Insights yellow' were more likely to indicate that they perceived 'considerable flexibility' or 'some flexibility', and were much less likely to indicate that they perceived 'no flexibility'.

- Those who had a higher score for 'Insights red' were more likely to indicate that they perceived 'considerable flexibility', and much less likely to indicate that they perceived either 'some flexibility' or 'no flexibility'.

There are two key implications in these findings that are worth highlighting. First, higher levels of agency (and particularly observations of considerable flexibility) were more likely to be observed in those who had an extroverted preference, while lower levels of agency (and particularly observations of no flexibility) were more likely to be observed in those who had an introverted preference. Secondly, those who had a thinking preference were more likely to indicate a perceived extreme of agency ('Insights blue' was more likely to perceive only 'no flexibility', and 'Insights red' was more likely to perceive only 'considerable flexibility'), while those who had a feeling preference were more likely to indicate a perceived range of agency ('Insights green' was more likely to perceive 'no flexibility' or 'some flexibility', while 'Insights yellow' was more likely to perceive 'some flexibility' or 'considerable flexibility').

The results of the comparison of agency with those of personality indicated a strong level of individual influence on agency. In addition to the structural influences of position and decision involvement, individual participant personalities appeared to strongly shape the degree to which they were likely to perceive themselves as having agency. The tendency of extroverted preferences towards greater levels of agency, and particularly for those who had a more extroverted-thinking ('Insights red') preference, suggests reinforcement of traits that are common to these preferences. As defined by

Jung (1971) and operationalized in Insights Discovery (British Psychological Society, 2009), extroverts tend to have a greater level of optimism, enthusiasm and confidence; in addition, those with an extroverted-thinking preference tend to be strongly independent-minded, goal-oriented, purposeful and driven. Extroverts are therefore more likely to have a greater level of confidence in their ability to make a difference, and extroverted-thinkers are more likely to be independent and to work within their own interpretation of the rules. The tendency of introverted preferences to perceive themselves as having lower levels of agency, and particularly for that of a more introverted-thinking ('Insights green') preference to do so, is also telling. As defined by Jung (1971) and operationalized in Insights Discovery (British Psychological Society, 2009), introverts tend to place a greater emphasis on traditional approaches, convention and perceived standards; those with an introverted-feeling preference in particular are sensitive to norms, conventions and the perceived expectations of others. Introverts are more likely to perceive constraints and cautions, and introverted-feelers are more likely to work within the guidelines and prescribed expectations of others. A key distinction highlighted by the influence of personality on agency is the behaviour that people adopt while performing the project shaper role: 'Would they be too quiet, are they going to stand up for themselves? Are they outgoing enough? Introverts don't really fit in here well, unless they are more in development roles, where they are more detailed. You've got to be seen here' (29).

While the characteristics of different personality preferences could certainly be suggested to have moderate alignment with the range of dimensions of agency described in this study, the degree to which this has actually been observed suggests that this influence is significant.

STATISTICAL COMPARISONS

As the Insights Discovery evaluator produces a quantitative component, an analysis of variance (ANOVA) of agency correlated to the Insights colour scores for the participants within the study was produced to evaluate the degree to which personality influences agency. ANOVA generally assumes a normal distribution, and the analysis here presumes a normal distribution (the scores for personality are typically expected to follow a normal distribution, and are assumed to be symmetrically distributed evenly around the mean; Cohen, 2008). Despite the fact that the overall number of study participants (n = 28) is typically too small to support statistical analysis, and therefore the relative power of the results is comparatively low, statistically significant results were none the less obtained within this study. Given that, even with this small sample, some statistical significance was observed in relating personality preference to agency, it was felt that this was worthy of inclusion. The results are illustrated in Figures 6.3 and 6.4.

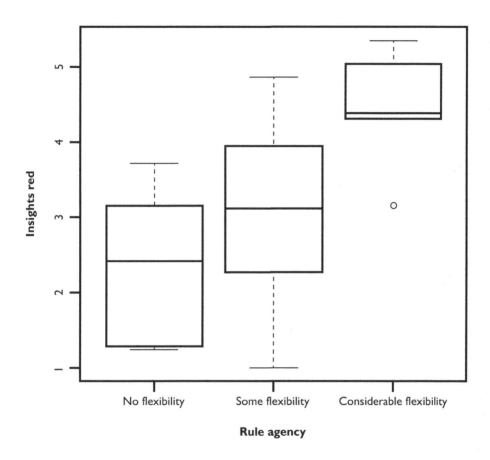

Figure 6.3   Rule agency versus 'Insights red' scores

While a multiple comparison of means does not show a statistical significance between 'no flexibility' and 'some flexibility', there is a statistically significant difference at a level of p = .05 between 'no flexibility' and 'considerable flexibility' (p = .0127). Those indicating a high level of agency in their organizations were far more likely to have a strong preference for 'Insights red'.

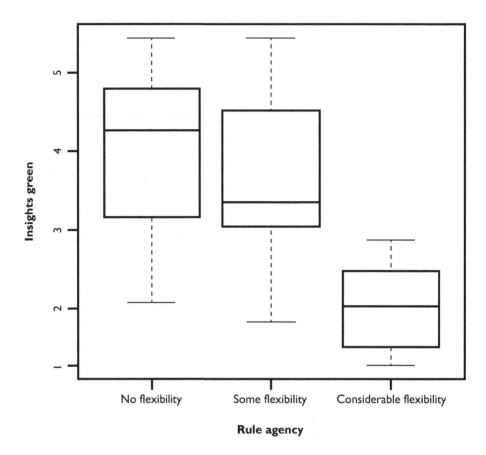

Figure 6.4   Rule agency versus 'Insights green' scores

In addition to the results for 'Insights red', there is also a significant result for 'Insights green' scores, which is the opposite preference of 'Insights red'. Again, there is no statistically significant result using a multiple comparison of means for 'no flexibility' and 'some flexibility', but there is a statistical difference for the comparison of both 'no flexibility' and 'considerable flexibility (p =.0113) and 'some flexibility' and 'considerable flexibility' (p = .0133). Even with a small sample size, these results continue to support a correlation between agency and personality. Participants indicating a high level of agency in their organizations were far more likely to have a low preference for 'Insights green', and conversely, those with a high preference for 'Insights green' were likely to indicate a lower level of agency, where they perceived no flexibility to influence the rule system of the organization.

Limitations on Individuals

Given the influence of agency on project initiation decisions, it is useful to understand the degree of agency that is actually being described and perceived by participants. Dietz & Burns (1992) suggested that four criteria need to be demonstrated in order to attribute agency to a social actor:

1. The agent must be able to 'make a difference' in exercising some sort of power over the situation.

2. The agent must be acting with intention in the situation.

3. The agent must have free play, meaning a range of possible actions, in a given situation.

4. The agent must be sufficiently reflexive to monitor the effects of their actions and be able to adjust their rule systems in response to previous actions.

In the context of the above criteria, arguably only those study participants who indicated considerable flexibility could be genuinely considered to be executing agency. Those participants who indicated only moderate levels of flexibility had some level of agency, but arguably there was less emphasis on at least the first and third criteria: they had less of a perception that their actions had an impact, and felt they had a more constrained range of possible actions from which to choose. Those participants who indicated that they had no flexibility in their approach did not meet any of the criteria; they did not indicate an ability to make a difference, they did not see that they had the ability to act with intent, they viewed their actions as constrained, and they perceived the rule system to be prescribed. While the concept of agency is strongly present in the findings, therefore, it is in the context of varying degrees of agency rather than an absolute understanding of the presence of agency. Some participants can be said to have fully operationalized the concept of agency as proposed by Dietz & Burns, others only exercised partial agency, and some perceived themselves as having no influence or flexibility in their actions at all. Therefore, given this range of practices within the domain of agency, there is a need to understand how different degrees of agency are in fact exercised, and what constitute the other influences on project initiation decisions.

The analysis thus far has explored the influences of agency on project initiation, the degree to which participants indicated that they had flexibility and the ability to influence the rules of project initiation, and the actions they took in interacting with those rules. A number of questions still remain, however, regarding the influence of agency on project initiation:

- Why did some participants with executive power not exhibit agency?

- Why did some rule environments seem not to require agency?

- Where did agency influence decision and rule environment?

- Why were there scenarios where agency did not seem to have an impact?

Case Study: Exercising Agency

The following scenario that illustrates the effective exercising of agency is drawn from a private sector example. The participant in this instance was a mid-management-level project consultant within a large firm in the pharmaceutical sector. The participant was employed within the information services division of the organization, and the types of projects reflected within this scenario were large-scale systems development and integration efforts. The participant's self-declared role was: 'Structuring projects so that they are technically feasible, tracking them to ensure that they remain there, and getting involved when projects run into trouble in order to get them back on track' (6).

In describing whether the organization focused on explicit or implicit rules, the participant's response was a clear rejection of both: 'My answer to that is "neither". Moving forward by the nature of the environment, neither the implicit social rules or the explicit required rules are sufficient to get projects approved. You need to go out of band for all of these' (6). In other words, getting projects initiated requires an established willingness to go outside of the rules.

Despite the professed requirement to work 'outside the system' to get projects initiated, there was a defined and relatively formal process in place governing the process of project initiation. The process was described as having 'some formality' and being 'mostly consistent', but at the same time was characterized by the participant as being 'not effective'. In discussing the process, the participant indicated:

Technically, you will always do the formal exercise. All of the documents will be produced, but the quality of the content of those documents is never really discussed in detail. Side discussions become dominant terms of whether the project gets approved, and after that they check for a positive NPV [net present value]. (6)

The perception of the process was that it was a vehicle that presumed moving to execution without any real consideration; it was a means of providing an on-paper justification for decisions that had already been made.

In performing the role of project shaper, the participant perceived a number of drivers as influencing her ability to be effective, including credibility and expertise. The initial basis of credibility was perceived as being a product of 'experience' and 'reputation':

The executive wants and is comfortable with a statement that is provided with 'moral confidence', that has clear expertise. That is not just whim. The ability of the person to be able to understand the details, where if they press, they will get a solid answer back. It helps if that person has a track record. (6)

In defining and initiating projects, however, the participant primarily emphasized a process of 'proactive communications', where she actively engaged with stakeholders who had an influence on or were impacted by the project. In describing the successful approach, the participant said:

I reach out to the organization that is concerned and involve them in the discussion and the decision making. I clearly listen to concerns. That is not the same as accepting demands, but it is involving them deeply enough in what is going on that they can realize themselves what the trade-offs are. (6)

While credibility and expertise were seen as being important in dealing with the executives, the participant credited a process of open communication as an honest broker and facilitator for success.

Politics was characterized as having 'strong influence' within the organization. Decisions were made at the senior executive committee, with strong input from Finance. The decision was: 'derived in principle based upon business analysis. No one will really know what the costs are, and no one really knows what the returns are. The process is flawed, but it is what all companies use' (6). At the same time, there was a very clear realization that politics was the means by which the participant exercised influence in supporting the project initiation process:

> *Politics at the level I mostly work on is in terms of the competing needs of various groups, and how well the project is going to meet those various needs. That's intrinsic – that's the problem. When I am doing a project I can do it to help this space, or that space. This becomes a critical conversation – too comprehensive, and the project becomes too big; too small, and it doesn't get done. (6)*

While the decision politics was seen as being arbitrary, the process of politics itself was the means by which the participant identified herself as being successful, and the essence of how she solved problems associated with an individual project.

The participant described the decision process within the organization as having 'insufficient process' and being 'arbitrary'. In describing how the initiation decision itself was made, she said: 'Slide discussions become dominant in terms of whether the project gets approved, and then they check for a positive NPV [net present value]. There is this informal process, because the document package as a whole doesn't provide understanding' (6). The participant's criticism of this process was that there was little understanding of what was actually being done within a project, and what would be produced as a result.

The role of the project shaper was seen as 'informal', and as traditionally played out, it was not necessarily effective. In discussing the shaper role, the participant said: 'It is a typical role, but not an official one. Technically supposed to be executive champion or business sponsor' (6). When addressed informally, however, a subject matter expert could have much more influence on the process: 'In practice, [a] member of the core team will come in who really understands the project – and if you can get that, it will succeed' (6). The shaper role was still important, but what was critical was having someone who actually understood the project and could advocate for what is required.

In terms of agency, this participant reported having 'considerable flexibility', and also considerable success:

> *My projects seldom fail. I can usually take the approach that I believe needs to occur to get traction. It often takes a long time to get the initial*

traction. But I understand how to work with the culture of most of the
sites – by nature that is where I started. (6)

An essential key to exercising agency was seen as understanding not what the rules were, but the underlying principles and limits that led to the rules being established in the first place:

Going back thirty years now, a key is to understand what the rules
are. Not what the full processes are, but the various limits. Why the
limits are there. What the expectation of those is. A lot of small projects
are much easier to succeed at than one large project. Structuring of
your projects, consistent with the governance rules of your company –
don't cheat here (don't make five $9,999 projects if the limit is $10,000).
Understand the rules and work within them. (6)

While the participant described her approach as working within the rules, it became clear from many examples that appeared in her contribution to the study that she often worked around them without violating the core principles the rules were based upon, and respecting and adhering to the cultural principles and values that existed within the organization.

As in the 'Case Study: Process Influences' in Chapter 4, a process governing project initiation was in place, and it was adhered to with relative consistency. Unlike the previous scenario, however, this process was not seen as providing a great deal of value, supporting comprehension of individual projects or leading to an effective decision making process. What compensated for this was the agency of the individual participant. She saw herself as having a great deal of latitude, flexibility and autonomy, and in part viewed the value of her role as being that of an 'iconoclast' with a reputation for actually getting things done. Despite ineffective politics, ineffective process and arbitrary decision making, strong agency in this case provided a means of navigating the project initiation process in such a way that projects could best be positioned for success.

This category of rule system does not occur at the intersection of rule emphasis and effectiveness, but in fact transcends several of them. Within the study, several participants indicated the presence of 'considerable flexibility', and with that flexibility, a strong level of agency. Five participants indicated strong levels of agency. While the underlying process effectiveness and rule effectiveness of the environments described by these participants were either 'somewhat effective' or 'not effective', these participants collectively described circumstances where the exercising of their personal level of agency was able to compensate for deficiencies within their organizations. The implication is that the presence of strong agency is sufficient to compensate for ineffective rule systems and process capabilities within the project initiation process.

The implications of the role of agency are significant. The construct of agency is one that is perceived within individuals; it is not a measure of broad flexibility within the organization itself. Individuals with strong agency have taken it upon themselves to circumvent, stretch, reinterpret or ignore various rules and processes in their organizations in order to support the projects they are working to initiate. Depending upon the organization, these actions may have been consciously sought, condoned or actively or passively ignored. While it is possible for agency to compensate for ineffective process or inappropriate rules, this is a product of the behaviours of individuals rather than organizations.

As has also been observed, where there are strong processes – defined as those that are very formal and very consistent – strong levels of agency do not appear to be required. Executives who in other contexts might have strong personal influence and autonomy indicate a suborning of this individual flexibility in favour of the organizational processes. Within these organizations, it is questionable what influence strong agency, of the nature that has been described here, would actually have. It is arguable that, particularly where the process continues to be seen as being effective, strong agency would be discouraged and suppressed as counter to the interests of the organization. Efforts to circumvent the rules would likely be constrained rather than condoned.

Conclusions

The concepts explored and expanded upon in this chapter collectively have a significant influence on how project initiation decisions are made, from the perspective of the participants in this study. They also describe the broad influence on the project initiation process of the exercising of agency. Collectively, the concepts that have been discussed in this chapter are those that are deemed to be essential influences on how project initiation decisions are being managed and influenced by individuals within the various participant organizations.

As discussed in this chapter, decision effectiveness is predominantly influenced by the exercise of agency, which is augmented by process effectiveness and rule effectiveness within an organization. Where there is a process emphasis within the organization, process effectiveness has an influence on overall decision effectiveness. Process effectiveness is itself influenced by process formality, process consistency, decision process formality and the exercising of process drivers of personal influence. Where there is an implicit emphasis within the organization, rule effectiveness has an influence on overall decision effectiveness. Rule effectiveness is itself influenced by the presence of political drivers of personal influence, and is negatively impacted by the presence of negative decision politics, and by the informality of the project shaper role. In all instances, the personal exercise of agency shapes the degree to which project initiation decisions are effective. The degree of agency that is exercised is a product of whether actors see themselves as being empowered as a result of their personal attributes, or constrained as a result of external factors. These relationships reflect the collective influences on how agency is exercised in project initiation decisions, and provides a basis for formulating a theory of how agency and rule emphasis influence project initiation decisions.

Chapter 7
When Choices Go Off the Rails

Introduction

While the previous three chapters have identified the degrees to which process, politics and personal agency can all play a significant role in determining the effectiveness of project initiation decisions, not all organizational environments are positive and not all initiation decisions are supported successfully. There are instances where the decision making environment is in fact very ineffective, and the factors that influence ineffectiveness are largely the same factors that influence successful decision making, but played out in reverse. Specifically, ineffective decision making environments are the product of inappropriate process, the lack of constructive politics and the failure of individuals to leverage agency effectively in supporting project initiation decisions.

This chapter explores examples of where decision making effectiveness is compromised or less effective than would normally be desired or appropriate. It highlights the challenges that are encountered in less than effective environments, why those challenges exist, and the consequences for decision making. It does so specifically through the exploration of three scenarios: where process and agency are insufficient, where processes are ineffective, and where politics is dysfunctional. A final case study also illustrates that even in the presence of dysfunction and the absence of agency, it is still possible to find strategies to get things done and to support effective decisions.

Case Study: When Process and Agency Struggle

This scenario evaluates the impact of a more explicit approach to project initiation, where neither process nor agency are fully able influence decision making effectiveness. The organization was a large international telecommunications firm. The participant was a senior project director within the information technology division of the organization. Typical projects were large-scale information systems, including the development of new technology-based customer services.

The emphasis of the rules system within the organization was described by the participant as mostly explicit. While there was an allowance for some implicit rules, and there was recognition that these had more influence in the past, the organization had evolved in terms of the rigour and scrutiny of project initiation decisions: 'Normally, implicit rules are more important. However, in today's environment, when the organization is looking for a reason to cancel or suspend projects, the explicit rules need to be rigorously followed. The explicit status of projects is too public' (24). The scrutiny that was a product of the current business environment had effectively served to increase the emphasis on explicit, tangible processes in decision making.

Given the explicit focus of the organization, there was also a fairly significant emphasis on the processes in place. The participant reported that the process environment had 'some formality': 'I think it is pretty formal in terms of governance panels. Initiation is not that formal, but we do have a governance committee, and a business case. Dollar level determines delegation levels' (24). In terms of consistency, the process environment was perceived as being very consistent: 'Now it is much more stringently controlled. Fifteen to twenty years ago, you would have seen much more discretionary projects' (24). While there was a reasonable degree of formality in place, the participant still described challenges where projects were initiated due more to political influences: 'There have been occasions where the vendor has come up with a wonderful solution, and then you go looking for a problem that it will solve' (24). Overall, however, there was a suggestion that there was a reasonable degree of formality and scrutiny in place governing how project initiation decisions were made.

In this context, the participant saw personal influence as primarily a product of diligence and proactive communications. While the participant was quite senior and in a technical role, there was less of an emphasis on knowledge than on a need to build understanding and consensus:

> *I draw boxes, and ask people to build systems to support them. I don't pretend to know the ins and outs. I meet with people, and ensure that I am seen to support them. If there are things that need to be sorted out, I will support them. If there are show stoppers, then we will work through those together. (24)*

The participant described his approach as: 'Initially, just asking questions. Presuming that I know nothing, and asking questions to try and get information and feedback. In identifying that I am starting at ground-zero level there is a tendency for people to be fairly supportive' (24). Credibility was seen as bringing process and knowledge to the table, but constantly framing it from the perspective of the people who were impacted, and based upon their needs.

In this organization, while there was process in place that was being increasingly emphasized, politics still exerted a strong influence. There was a strong need for political acceptance and to seek buy-in in order for projects to be initiated:

> *You need to have a champion at a high level. Have to do that, and then they can talk to and liaise with their peers, socialize issues, get buy-in. The higher level the buy-in, the greater likelihood that solution will be accepted. Makes it harder to oppose. (24)*

Acceptance of projects was seen as a product of both process adherence and political acceptance. Describing the influence of politics, the participant reported:

> *If you don't have support across the organization then there is a good chance that the project could be in jeopardy if you don't have all your ducks lined up. In other words, you need the formal admin support (a funded business case and current status in green) as well as peer and/ or senior management support, for example due to strategic value. (24)*

The politics in this organization essentially worked hand-in-hand with the process, and both had to be respected and supported.

The decision process in this organization was committee-based. As described by the participant, this also had political dimensions, where approval 'would be done at governance committee. It is usually brought forward by the project sponsor that has asked you to run the study. There is a need to get buy-in beforehand; they would liaise with other members before meeting' (24). The political interactions were not always supportive: 'Sometimes someone lobs a bomb in; sometimes the sponsor themselves' (24). The implication was that despite the professed formality, the decision process itself was still subject to a great deal of political influence.

Within this organization, the role of project shaper was recognized as the task of a sponsor. There was a clear need to have a high-level champion of the project, particularly if there was some risk associated with the project. Recruiting executives into the project shaper role was also subject to political considerations. Discussing the shaper role, the participant said: 'I think they have to be sold to it, it can't be imposed. If they are not sold on it, then they can't champion it. They have to see what the benefits are; you don't want a reluctant champion' (24). The role of champion in this context was important, but the project shaper had to be someone who clearly understood and accepted the benefits before they could champion those benefits to others.

In this scenario, the agency of the participant was identified as having some flexibility. While this individual was confident in his credibility, there was a very high level of awareness of the power structure and the politics that existed within the organization. The participant had an appreciation of the process that was in place, and the need to be seen to be adhering to that process. He also recognized the role politics played in the initiation of projects and the on-going maintenance of project support. However, it was not the influence or power of the participant that drove this support; support was sustained by working within the process and political environment that was established and maintained by others.

While he did not have political influence, the participant did engage in supporting and stewarding the project through the initiation process for those projects for which he was responsible. The participant brought a strong level of technical and managerial competence, while emphasizing the needs and priorities of stakeholders during the performance of their role. The consultative process, which was highlighted, was very much based on developing workable and technically appropriate solutions that met stakeholder requirements.

This scenario illustrates how moderate levels of agency and adherence to process, as well as to politics, can still produce moderately effective results. The characteristics that are common to cases such as this one encompass both organizational and personal dimensions. The process environment in these types of organizations was characterized as having some formality and some consistency. While the process of project initiation was not extremely formal, there was a process in place that was adhered to reasonably well on at least a subset of projects. The other predominant characteristic, however, was how those who were guiding and shaping their projects approached their roles. What participants in the project shaper role described was an emphasis on the process drivers of influence, namely diligence, experience, process and reputation. In other words, they reinforced what process was in place with their own personal emphasis on rigour and process. While not all of the participants here had agency, and those who did characterized it as having only some flexibility, they worked within the process and reinforced and emphasized the process through their own behaviours.

Case Study: Ineffective Processes

This scenario explores the implications of the absence of process. The organization was a department within a Canadian provincial government. The participant was a director responsible for a major programme area within the department. The organization typically undertook projects to develop, revise and assess programmes in support of the departmental mandate.

The participant identified the rule emphasis within the organization as mostly implicit. This was largely a result of the lack of clear rules in terms of project initiation within the organization. When asked to describe how familiar with the rules they were, the participant responded: 'That's hard to answer, because I just transitioned. But fairly well – because there aren't a lot' (2). There were aspects of process in place, and a project management office has been established within the organization, but there was not a great deal of formal process guidance governing the initiation process.

In terms of process, the organization was described as having little formality. The participant described the organization as struggling with the initiation process, suggesting it was:

> Not formal at all. The first formal part is a project charter. A lot of times, the initiation decision has been made prior to doing the project charter. Sometimes the charter is used as the idea document, but a lot of times, 'Here's an idea and run with it.' We don't have a lot of great processes – formal processes – around project initiation. (2)

The process was also described as very inconsistent. In describing the initiation process, the participant indicated it was: 'Probably all over the map. A lot of times we will get told to do something because the premier/deputy/executive said so, and therefore we have to do it' (2). What process did exist focused more on formality of project management once a project has been initiated, rather than at the initiation stage. The implication was that while there was a stated intention of process, actual adherence was poor, and the manner in which projects were initiated was largely ad hoc.

In terms of discussing personal influence on the process, the participant particularly highlighted process-based drivers. The primary emphasis in influencing the process was placed on diligence, reputation and position. Many of the criteria for success were perceived to concern having done the preparatory work necessary to respond to challenges and issues: 'Being prepared, doing your homework, anticipating the sorts of questions that might be asked and being prepared for that type of thing' (2). Credibility was in part afforded by position and title, as well as informal and formal collaboration with peers. The consequences were that most of the effort was invested in making sure that due diligence had been done to address challenges and deficiencies, drawing on personal expertise and ability to navigate what process did exist as well as possible.

In addition to informal process, the participant described an organization that had a fairly significant level of politics. She indicated that politics had a strong influence: 'Tends to have quite a bit. A lot of it is timing related to other projects, and other priorities. Whether pressures become high enough that we may need to work on this' (2). In addition, there could be executive direction regarding what projects would actually be initiated; in discussing the need for executive support for a major initiative, the participant indicated: 'You need an ADM [assistant deputy minister], you need the deputy minister. If it is a level higher, if the deputy says we are doing it, then it will get done, whether supported or not' (2). In this context, political and executive priorities had the greatest influence, and what process did exist might easily be circumvented.

The decision making process was by consensus, where the executive led. The discussion involved reviewing a completed presentation, and a decision was often made in the room: 'The last slide is the decision. The deputy would lead the discussion with ADMs. The response is either that they need to think and discuss and get back to you, or the decision could be made right in the meeting (more typical in my experience)' (2).

The decision making process was also unclear, in large part as a result of a recent reorganization of the department. What decision making process did exist was not overly formal, with the participant indicating there was: 'Not great decision tracking; or even writing decisions down' (2). Decisions were made through verbal commitments that were not tracked, and for which no formal record might exist.

The role of project shaper was one that was recognized predominantly as the purview of a subject matter expert. In discussing the project shaper role, the participant said: 'Yes, it's the work that we do. There is a significant amount that is driven top-down. But there is also bottom-up initiation, given pressures' (2). People were predominantly assigned to the role based upon position, or based upon topic expertise. However, there was not always a great deal of support for people in the project shaper role: 'A lot of people are heads down. Not that there is an ill will, but people don't necessarily spend a lot of time thinking about what other people need' (2). The consequence was an environment where the shaper role, while recognized, was challenged in terms of obtaining credibility and support.

Given the organizational context to date, it is perhaps surprising that in terms of agency this participant identified some flexibility. In large part this was a result of the lack of rules and lack of formality of process, particularly with respect to the initiation process. At the same time, however, agency was constrained by the top-down and political nature that characterized so much of the organization's functions, and the imperatives that could frequently be established at executive level. Alignment was important, and results were important, but there was flexibility in how people went about doing that: 'If you don't use the right form, that's OK. If you do a 2.5-page briefing note, they will likely still read it' (2). Overall, there was a level of latitude that could be leveraged, provided one understood and worked within the organizational and political constraints.

While the participant exhibited some agency, it was within a very narrow context, and more importantly, was limited by a number of other considerations within the organization. The lack of a clear decision making process, the lack of process consistency and minimal formality of process conspired to create a process environment that was characterized as not effective. While the participant could attempt to either influence or work around this environment, the level of top-down influence and the tendency to either impose or override decisions meant that the overall impact of agency was negligible, and might only result in frustration on her part.

Within organizations characterized as having an explicit process environment but where the project initiation process is not effective, there appear to be a number of contributing characteristics. Three organizations were identified as having an explicit emphasis, while the actual process in place was characterized by participants as not effective. One was a government department, and the other two organizations were in the education sector.

The characteristics that predominate in these circumstances all highlight process challenges. The process environment is described as having little formality and no consistency. In other words, while there is a stated emphasis on applying formality in the process of project initiation, there is no process in place, nor is there any resulting consistency. In addition, the process of decision making in these instances is arbitrary and unclear. There is again a variation in agency, with participants indicating little or no flexibility, and what flexibility is available is insufficient to compensate for the inadequacies and organizational challenges that appear to exist. The ineffectiveness of the process constrains the ability for even some agency to have a lasting and significant influence.

Case Study: Dysfunctional Politics

While the previous scenario dealt with constrained agency and a lack of process, this scenario unwraps the influence of a lack of politics on project initiation. The organization was a large North American university. The participant was a senior project manager within the information technology group of the business school, who was responsible for supporting the initiation and subsequent management of systems development and implementation projects.

The rule environment within the organization was mostly implicit. While there was theoretically a formal process, much of the project initiation process was still responsive to implicit drivers:

> *I feel that the rules of the game are fluid in my organization. We're using a more formal approval process now, but even with that I feel that projects are selected based on who has more political influence rather than on which project will have greatest impact on the organization. (26)*

Even while recognizing the influence of politics, there was a level of idealism regarding adopting a more formal process. Discussing the importance of understanding rules, the participant said: 'It is more important to understand and adhere to the explicit rules. Our explicit rules call for formal project initiation processes. As we use the formal processes more often we'll be in a better position to change the implicit rules' (26). The implication here was that politics did in fact currently drive the project initiation process; at the same time, the participant hoped that process would supplant the politics.

While there was theoretically a formal process of project initiation, the organization was described as having some formality. In discussing the process, the participant indicated:

> *It is kind of in the middle of the road in terms of formality. Getting the business case, and producing project charters and plans. It is not as formal as it could be; we are not making decisions purely based upon the business need. Politics has a much higher ranking in terms of the decision. (26)*

In terms of consistency, the process was considered very consistent. While the process itself was not formal, there was at least adherence to it, with everything that met the definition of a project being subject to the process. Overall, however, the process was described as being not effective. The participant suggested: 'If it was a truly formal process, I would like think the documentation was more used in having a final say' (26). Even through there was theoretically a process in place, in this context it was clear that it was not being used, and that the influence of politics had a much greater role than process in evaluating projects and determining which ones proceeded.

In terms of personal drivers of influence, the participant highlighted those associated with reputation and diligence, while recognizing the need for proactive communication. There was again an effort to establish a core sense of credibility, of experience working on previous similar projects. The participant's personal approach in demonstrating influence was characterized as: 'Investigate the heck out of what the project will be. Be able to make insights that some people might not expect, and demonstrate an understanding of the business side. Technical credibility is not an issue, it is about demonstrating business understanding' (26).

While seeking to demonstrate understanding and insight, the participant also indicated that communications were managed carefully: 'I tend to manage how I give out information about the project; I may not be honest about my unhappiness, for example' (26). The clear emphasis for the participant was on being able to demonstrate expertise through credibility and diligence; at the same time, there was a tangible frustration that process was not being adequately valued.

In discussing the role of politics, and its 'strong influence' within this organization, the participant said:

> *Also a lot of the politics influences process. It drives me crazy, but instead of looking at the merits of the project my supervisor will look at the political power of the people requesting, and decide based upon power to proceed, even if it is not the best use of our time. If, for example, a request comes from the dean, it is more likely to proceed. (26)*

While there was a clear and stated desire on the part of the participant to make decisions based upon process and a thorough analysis of the problem: 'Politics has a much higher ranking in terms of the decision' (26). The implication of this was that there was a disconnect between the preferred approach of the participant and the political reality that existed within the organization. While there was a sense of optimism about the possibility of process to 'fix' the politics, the influence of politics was clearly far greater.

The decision process within the organization was relatively formal, and would be conducted by the board of trustees. The decision making process was also identified as an issue in terms of its impact on the project initiation process:

> *The decision would be made, but the board isn't affected by what doesn't happen. There is no consideration of the consequences of what will not happen as a result of making a particular decision. Board members are outside of the School – they are not affected by what wouldn't get done. (26)*

The implication was that each project was viewed in isolation, and approved on its own merits, with no consideration of the larger impacts. There was no assessment of the impact of not doing another project, or the overall resource impacts of the projects that were initiated.

The project shaper role was seen as at best informal in the context of this organization. In discussing whether a shaper role existed, the participant observed: 'No. Typically not. It is not there formally, but it might be informal. It is more looking at it on the technology side, less business analysis' (26). The implication was that there was no formal role that was responsible for advocacy or influence of the project within the organization.

In this scenario, the agency of the participant was described as having no flexibility. There was little influence in the project initiation process, nor in what was ultimately considered in making initiation decisions. In discussing how initiation occurred in actuality, the participant said: 'Implicitly, meetings with supervisor regarding the desired project. You have to win him over. Once you've won him over, it typically goes ahead, even if other things don't line up' (26). Politics was exercised and influence maintained by other people, and decisions were made regardless of their underlying logic or the impact a decision had on other work or projects in the organization. The participant not only did not influence this process, but indicated a sense of powerlessness and frustration with how the process actually operated.

While there was a strong sense that the participant held ideals regarding how project initiation should happen and the role process should play, these aspects ultimately did not influence the initiation of projects in this organization.

Politics and relationships were what governed project initiation, not analysis and rigour. Despite this, however, the participant strove to emphasize rigour and competence in supporting the initiation of projects, despite the fact that these were apparently not the drivers that were valued. This was a scenario where lack of agency, resentment of politics and a lack of influence on the process resulted in a project initiation process that was viewed as not effective, and that was a source of personal frustration for the participant.

Several characteristics appear to contribute in organizations that have an implicit rule system that is not seen to be effective. Nine organizations were described as having an implicit rule environment and a rule system that was not effective. These included four organizations in the education sector, two insurance companies, one financial firm, one retail organization and one aerospace firm.

The characteristics that predominated in this instance were a product of organizational as well as individual influences. Overall, these organizations were described as having political environments characterized by avoidance and disagreement. In addition, the role of project shaper in all of these organizations was described as being informal. Finally, the participants identified their level of agency as having no flexibility. The consequence was a situation with ineffective organizational politics, in which individual support in guiding project initiation was not formally recognized and participants indicated no personal influence or capacity to compensate for the inadequacies of the organization.

What is possibly most important to note about the presence of avoidance politics or an informal shaper role, however, is that where these are both present, they appear to override the influence of factors within the organization that otherwise would be characterized as having an implicit emphasis and being somewhat effective. In other words, the presence of an avoidance political culture and an informal shaper role are sufficient to counter the influence of agency and political drivers that might otherwise support an effective project initiation decision.

Case Study: When Agency is Not Enough

The examples that have been illustrated so far, and the theoretical framework that has emerged as a result, are all strongly supported by the majority of participant descriptions that were collected as a part of conducting this study.

As Corbin & Strauss (2008) point out, not all theories are perfect, and at times cases will exist that do not support, or in fact will refute, the data within a study. In their words: 'Looking for the negative case provides for a fuller exploration of the dimensions of a concept. It adds richness to explanation and points out that life is not exact and that there are always exceptions to points of view' (Corbin & Strauss, 2008, p. 84). So it is with this study, where there is one negative case which not only refutes one basis of theory, but also helps to illuminate and further explain how a portion of the theory may in fact operate (and indeed, may be able to be overcome).

The case in question concerns a participant who was a director within a North American university. He was a member of the executive team within his department, reporting directly to the dean, and was responsible for the initiation and oversight of all of the projects conducted within that department.

The emphasis of the rule environment within the organization was described as implicit; there were, in fact, very few written procedures or processes regarding project initiation. As a result, the processes were described as having little formality and moderate consistency. Politics had a strong influence, and was described by the participant as: 'Absolutely huge. Worse on some, but absolutely in all' (22). The politics was also heavily culturally influenced, and placed great emphasis on collaboration, consultation and accommodating individual viewpoints. In the words of the participant: 'You need to work and build a consensus – try to appease different points of view. Understand objectives and motivations. Most people will move off their point at times and see a larger good. It makes it extremely difficult when starting projects involving faculty' (22).

A strong level of avoidance was also characterized within the political environment. The decision environment was one where the dean of the department ultimately decided: 'He does try to get consensus. Would look for general agreement. But ultimately, if he says yes, it is a go' (22). The role of project shaper was varied; it was moderately formally recognized, but also described as involving a number of challenges: 'It's a diverse group – there may be people initially supportive, and some who aren't. The champion will have to work with all of the various groups to try and build consensus' (22). The level of agency was described as one of no flexibility. Overall, the implicit emphasis, lack of agency, presence of avoidance politics and the relatively informal role of project shaper would suggest that this organization be characterized as not effective. However, there were factors in place within this case that made the results more effective than a surface description of the organization might suggest.

The difference in this case was how the participant in this scenario approached the project shaper role. The environment the participant described was a difficult one politically. In discussing the politics within the organization, the participant reported that it: 'can be extremely challenging. As administration, I'm a second class citizen' (22). This person's observations on the importance of working within the rules are also relevant: 'In this environment, I can't get into anything but trouble by initiating something on my own, without consensus and agreement of my colleagues' (22). Despite the perception of minimal agency and the relatively difficult and obstructive environment, however, the participant in this scenario had found strategies to be effective in his role.

The significance of the approach this particular participant adopted is highlighted by the drivers of personal influence he identified. There was an emphasis on 'reputation', which was defined less as a track record of technical expertise than an emphasis on personal integrity: 'Being very careful to try to keep personal integrity. One of the things I find – be careful about, if promising something, make sure that you can deliver on it. Don't try to get yourself in a position where you are making conflicting promises to different people' (22).

The participant engaged in proactive communications, which in part meant: 'I will listen a lot' (22). There was a dimension of political savvy, characterized as: 'Very careful not to push, not to embarrass, keep plugging away' (22). In describing his approach, the participant indicated:

> *I think people have different ways. In my case ... quiet persistence.*
> *I will listen a lot. I will look for things that can be done to help. Work to*
> *make their life a little bit easier. Help do what we need to do. Make sure*
> *we deliver or over-deliver. (22)*

Despite an organization that could be considered very negative, and despite the lack of agency or perception of any flexibility, the participant had found a strategy to make things work and move from being not effective to being at least somewhat effective through an approach that can best be described – to use his own words – as quiet persistence.

The importance of this negative case is that it reinforces that there is in fact another dimension of personal influence than just agency in how people approach the project shaper role; there is also a question of the strategies they adopt, and the personal drivers underlying those strategies. While the influence of the personal drivers is highlighted in the theoretical framework outlined earlier, there they are presented in a context where personal drivers of influence augment agency. In this particular example, personal drivers of influence in fact compensated for a lack of agency. What the theoretical framework suggests should be a less effective environment was compensated for by the personal approach of an individual who cared enough to work to make a difference despite the constraints he faced.

Factors Limiting Agency

While strategies for effectively and responsibly employing agency are a significant part of the theoretical framework resulting from this study, there is also a reality that agency has been limited or constrained in several scenarios as well. There are organizational and individual considerations for where this has occurred. In having a full appreciation of the role of agency in project initiation decisions, it is important to understand both of them.

From an organizational perspective, agency was described as being constrained or limited in two specific instances: those organizations described as having the most formal processes, and those that had the least. In organizations where the process was very formal and very consistent, agency was described as being less necessary, and could be argued to be counter to the intended objectives of having in place a well-defined process to which the organization consistently adhered. When the rules were formally defined and intended to be consistently adhered to, willingness to operate around or outside the rules could be considered counterproductive behaviour.

The other instance of agency being constrained by organizational factors emerged predominantly within implicit rule systems with a negative political environment, and where the project shaper role was seen as informal. Even in instances where the actor described a level of agency characterized as 'some flexibility', the presence of an avoidance political culture and insufficient recognition of the shaper role were enough to negate the impacts of agency that otherwise should have been possible. The implication of this is that there are some organizational environments that are sufficiently caustic and obstructive in terms of politics that those with only 'some' levels of agency are unable to make a difference. While strong levels of agency may be sufficient to overcome organizational inertia, as evidenced in other participant descriptions, there is a delicate balance between the forces of agency and avoidance. While someone with sufficient agency may be successful in supporting initiation of a project, there is also the risk that an organizational environment may have sufficiently negative and obstructive politics that efforts to exercise agency may be actively suppressed, or the exercise of agency may be personally dangerous or career-limiting.

The final considerations concerning limitations of agency are personal in nature. Just as there was a positive correlation of agency and personality, there was also a negative one, and it had the greatest level of statistical significance in the study findings. Those with the lowest scores of 'Insights green' were most likely to be characterized as having agency described as 'strong flexibility'; those with high scores of 'Insights green' were most likely to be characterized as having agency described as only exhibiting 'some flexibility' or 'no flexibility'. The study findings also demonstrated that those with the lowest levels of agency attributed this to external constraints, while those with the highest levels of agency attributed this to personal capabilities. It is arguable, based upon these findings, that these attributions may be simply perceptions. The level of agency, the capacity to be flexible and to flexibly and creatively respond to situations, may be largely a product of how much actors feel they are able to exercise it.

Conclusions

As this chapter has illustrated, while agency can be a powerful force for action in supporting the initiation of projects, sometimes it is not enough. The preceding chapters illustrated examples where agency supported – and in some instances compensated for – inadequacies in the processes and rule systems of organizations. In this chapter, the presence of agency struggled to compensate for ineffective approaches within the organization. While in some instances it was possible to still muddle through and realize an acceptable outcome, in other organizations either ineffective processes or dysfunctional politics conspired to prevent effective initiation decisions from being made. This serves to highlight an important consideration: while agency can be useful, and can compensate for organizational adequacies, there are circumstances where this is still not sufficient to ensure decision making effectiveness. Whether because of the organization's dysfunctions or individuals' failures to optimize their influence, decisions are ineffective and the organization fails to thrive. While agency has emerged from this research as a significant force in influencing decision making effectiveness, it is not a panacea. There are circumstances where it can help, certainly; however, there also situations where attempting to exercise agency can be counterproductive and career-limiting. Assessing the organization appropriately and evaluating the capacity and latitude to take independent action are critical for any individual who seeks to champion the launch of a new initiative.

Chapter 8
Shaping Better Project Results

Introduction

While the stories, examples and illustrations explored in the previous chapters each have their own fascinations, either as exemplary role model or cautionary tale, by this point the reader will inevitably be asking the question, 'So how do I apply this?' Answering this question is a multi-part proposition. As I have demonstrated so far, effective project initiation is a product of the intersection between the culture of the organization and the role of the individual. For individuals to act effectively, they need to understand their environment, and have an appreciation of the political and process dynamics that are at play. They also require a level of personal mastery in how they present and manage information within their organizations in support of getting projects initiated. Most importantly, they need to make relevant judgements about how to appropriately support decisions and take action in order to get projects initiated effectively. In the next three chapters, we will explore the practical implications of what has been discussed thus far. This chapter focuses on how those who find themselves in the project shaper role – by accident or design – can best support the project initiation process. It explores how to develop and reinforce agency as a mechanism for supporting or compensating for organizational inadequacies, what to look for in evaluating the organization and devising the most relevant strategy to move forward, and guidelines for embracing the project shaper role.

Developing Agency

The presence of agency has been identified in several instances as having a positive influence on the effectiveness of the rule environments within organizations. The presence of 'strong agency' has been demonstrated to compensate for a range of political and process-related challenges. It has had a positive influence in organizations where the rule system has been described as 'somewhat effective'. Its absence has in part contributed to the identification of rule systems as being 'not effective'. Perhaps most importantly, it is one of the few genuinely personal influences on the initiation process within organizations.

As identified earlier in this study, the influences on agency that have emerged are predominantly threefold:

1.   position within the organization;

2.   influence on the decision;

3.   personality of the project shaper.

Of the characteristics that have been identified, two are predominantly a consequence of the organizational structure and power dynamics within the organization, and there is little personal room for movement. While individuals can strive to elevate themselves within the organizational hierarchy, this is a long-term endeavour and subject to a number of personal and organizational considerations. Given the association of decision influence with positional authority, enhancement of this influence in this factor is equally tied to elevation in the organization. While promotion will have an influence over time, it is a long-term method of developing agency.

The other characteristic influencing agency, the personality of the project shaper, is interesting. The findings of this study identified a strong correlation between an agency of 'considerable flexibility' and high scores in the personality dimension of 'Insights red', which is predominantly associated with extroverted-thinking. The characteristics of 'Insights red' behaviour – confidence, assertiveness, goal-orientation and outcome focus – are certainly ones that correlate with the concept of high levels of agency. It reflects a willingness and confidence on the part of an individual to step out and face challenges. Those with strong scores in 'Insights red' are more likely to see success as a product of their individual contributions and efforts.

At the same time, there was also a reasonably strong correlation between an agency of 'considerable flexibility' and low scores in the personality dimension of 'Insights green', which is predominantly associated with introverted-feeling. The characteristics of 'Insights green' behaviour – support for others, desire for harmony, caution, resistance to change – are also ones that are less likely to be associated with perceptions of high levels of agency. It reflects more of an emphasis on reliance on others and caution in the face of challenge.

Those with high scores in 'Insights green' would be more likely to be conscious of and constrained by perceived external barriers and limitations.

While changing personality in order to enhance agency may seem to be a strong prescription, awareness of these aspects of personality – and their influence on agency – is important. As noted earlier, those with the strongest levels of agency viewed their success as a product of individual capabilities, latitude and influence, while those with the lowest levels of agency highlighted the influence of external forces as constraints. The implication of this insight is not that those with an 'Insights red' personality genuinely have more personal influence or that those with an 'Insights green' personality have more external constraint; it is that each of these personalities perceives this reality. The orientation of 'Insights red' is more inclined to place emphasis on their personal qualities and capabilities, while an orientation of 'Insights green' is more inclined to place emphasis on external barriers and roadblocks, or reliance on structural processes and structures.

Part of the challenge of developing agency, then, is a product of orientation. If we approach a problem focused on limitations and barriers, those are what we are most likely to observe; if we approach a problem focused on opportunities for success, those are what we are most likely to realize. While personality is perceived to be relatively fixed, at least in terms of core preferences, this study suggests that individuals who are able to enhance confidence, self-reliance and a belief in the existence and effectiveness of their capabilities are more likely to perceive themselves as having greater agency than those who do not or cannot.

Considerations in Employing Agency

While the development or enhancement of levels of personal agency is one challenge facing individuals who find themselves in the role of project shaper, the effective employment of agency also requires focus and consideration. While agency represents the degree of personal flexibility and autonomy individuals possess and are willing to exercise within and around the rule system in their organization, how agency is employed has been demonstrated to influence whether the resulting process or rule system is perceived as being effective or not. The responsible exercise of agency would also therefore seem to be an important consideration for individuals in the project shaper role.

An important first step in exercising agency is to understand the rule system that exists within the organization. Understanding the rule system requires being aware of both the political and the process dimensions of the project initiation process, and the degree to which each is adhered to within the organization. As has been observed in the various participant descriptions within this study, there are varying degrees of adherence to the process of project initiation. The type of project, its urgency, the status and relative power of the sponsor, the effectiveness of politics within the executive team and the wielding of executive fiat have all been demonstrated to influence how projects are initiated and the degree to which they conform to the stated processes and rules within the organization. Recognizing the formality, consistency and actual application of the rule system associated with project initiation is therefore an important initial step.

Equally important is understanding the emphasis of the rule system within the organization. This means understanding whether there is more of an orientation towards explicit process, implicit understanding, or a combination of the two. The mere presence of process is not necessarily an indication in this regard; what must be determined is the degree to which the process is actually utilized, with what level of formality and rigour, and by whom. As noted earlier, some participants described the emphasis in their organization as being 'explicit' because that was how they personally desired the rule system to operate, whereas the actual operation of the rule system was far more implicit, being driven largely by political influence. Recognition of whether the rule system is genuinely explicit, implicit or a variation is also necessary in understanding how to exercise agency.

Exercising agency in a manner that is appropriate would therefore appear to be a product of emphasizing the aspects of agency that have the greatest influence depending upon the context of the rule system and its emphasis. Where there is an implicit focus, exercising agency, and in particular reinforcing collaborative and political aspects of behaviour, would appear to be appropriate; this would include leveraging relationships, communicating proactively and being sensitive to the political dynamics and influences at work within the project initiation decision. Where there is an explicit focus, emphasizing the process dimensions of influence appears to be more effective: exercising diligence, demonstrating expertise, reinforcing process and underlining the track record of the project shaper in similar previous efforts. Where there are characteristics associated with rule systems that have been seen as 'not effective', it would also appear to be important to recognize that the only compensating influence may be the agency – and its relative strength – of the individual in the project shaper role. Depending upon the degree of politics, and the extent to which it is negative and hostile or the role of project shaper is not formally recognized, an individual may still be unsuccessful.

A final consideration in discussing the responsible exercising of agency concerns where there is in place a very formal, very consistent process. In these situations, the process is the basis of the rule system, and there is clearly a strong level of investment in establishing and sustaining that rule system. In such a context, exercising agency may not only be inappropriate, but could also be counterproductive. It is a telling observation that none of the participants who described such an environment indicated that they utilized a considerable level of agency, and those who exercised any agency were very clear about the contexts and situations in which it was appropriate. Strong agency and strong process capabilities are therefore potentially not compatible.

Taking Organizational Action

So what does it mean to exercise agency and take organizational action in initiating projects? It is important to acknowledge that it means stepping out and taking action that might be considered risky by some. Any action that is taken independently rather than being arrived at by simply following the rules and conventions of the organization could on some level be considered risky. That is not to say that it *is* risky, or that it is not the right thing to do. What it means is that we are taking personal responsibility for an action because we believe that it is appropriate and necessary. That action will have its supporters who believe that the action is required and needs to be embraced. The action will also inevitably have its detractors who believe that the action is inappropriate, undesirable, not valued and possibly even counterproductive. Arguably, this is the case with all organizational change: actions will be supported by some, opposed by others, and have an impact only if there is a critical mass of commitment to the action being taken.

While the concept of agency plays a significant role in the results of the research described in this book, it is not a new concept. Indeed, the exploration of the interaction between personal freedom and the constraints of organizational rules and structures has been a broad theme and a source of on-going debate amongst institutional theorists. This debate has tended to be framed by two camps, with one side arguing for increasing isomorphism of organizations, where rules and structures in an industry or context are expected to broadly align and resemble each other over time, and the other side arguing for agency as a vehicle for discretion in approaches through acts of deviance or institutional entrepreneurship (Heugens & Lander, 2009). The idea that agency can be viewed as on one hand an 'act of deviance' and on the other hand an act of 'institutional entrepreneurship' is an intriguing one, as there are inherent value judgements being made in both cases. If characterized as deviance, the actions are largely painted with a negative brush as unwanted, unhelpful and disruptive. The idea of institutional entrepreneurship, however, offers a far more positive and encouraging perspective. It suggests that agency is a positive force for change in the face of unhelpful, archaic and ossified organizational structures. The challenge is that these perspectives are not formed by the actor who is endeavouring to exercise agency; they are judgements of the organizational culture, and reflect in part how successful an actor is likely to be in exercising agency.

One other aspect of agency highlighted by this study is the level at which it is exercised. The project initiation process is unique in that it lives in a middle space between organizational strategy and project management; before project initiation comes the development of strategic direction, and after initiation exists the often rational and control-oriented processes of project management. As has been demonstrated in this study, some actors in the project shaper role are at executive levels, although not all of these exhibit high levels of agency; many, however, are at a mid-management or project management level in their organization, and yet are still charged with stewarding the initiation of strategically important initiatives. This raises interesting perspectives, and suggests the presence of agency at a different level of the organizational structure than that at which it has more traditionally been examined.

The traditional perspective on agency theory is that it involves executive- and board-level dynamics. A survey of agency theory literature highlighted that the dominant traditional focus of agency studies was on influences of executive compensation, behaviours of self-interest, and organizational dynamics – particularly with respect to executive motivation (Eisenhardt, 1989a). The tendency is towards a dominant viewpoint of executives as being those who typically exercise agency, in their role as agents who are accountable to principals that are typically represented by the board. By contrast, this study has identified the existence and operational use of agency at much lower levels of the organization, including in mid-level and project-based management. One of the closest alignments of the findings of this study with recent empirical discussions is that of Martynov (2009), who explored the dynamics of agency and stewardship in emphasizing managerial self-interest over stewardship and organizational interests; however, Martynov suggested that those acting as 'agents' operated from a self-interested perspective rather than serving organizational self-interests. This contrasts with the findings of this study, where those exercising the highest levels of agency in supporting the initiation of projects were doing so to help ensure that organizational interests were promoted, and in the process compensating for inadequacies in organizational processes and rule systems. Possibly most relevant to the study are the findings of Miller & Sardais (2011), who explored the role of executives in adopting stewardship approaches that were more generally associated with organizational principles. What this study demonstrates is that those exercising the greatest degree of agency are most commonly adopting a role of stewardship that aligns with the observations of Miller & Sardais (2011), but that the exercise of significant levels of agency is not solely at the executive level; it is also exercised by those in a mid-level or project management role.

Therefore, for any individuals taking action in an organization, it is essential to take stock of the culture and rule system of that organization. They need to be comfortable that they understand how it works, in the context of 'how things get done here'. They need to be confident that the action that is being considered is positive, necessary and aligned with the interests and overall objectives of the organization (while recognizing that it may well run into opposition and resistance in the short-term). They need to believe that they have both the freedom and the responsibility to act in the best interests of the organization, even where those actions may not be explicitly (or implicitly) coded in the rule system of the organization (and may in fact be contrary to them). In other words, they need to be comfortable taking independent action in the interests of the organization because doing so is the right thing to do.

Embracing the Role of Project Shaper

Smith & Winter (2010) define the project shaping role as one of sensemaking. Referring to the work of Weick (1995), they describe sensemaking as being rooted in identity construction, the interpretation of sensible environments that are social in nature and driven by a plausible understanding of cues within the environment. In the context of project shaping, the role is then interpreted as 'those acts performed by individuals to make that form of 'sense' that constitutes a new project' (Smith & Winter, 2010, p. 48). The framework that emerged from an analysis of their case narratives comprised six influences on project initiation, identified in the following points:

1. control model of projects;

2. tribal power;

3.   transformation and value;

4.   enacted reality;

5.   external dynamics – 'peripety';

6.   shapers' volition.

Within the current study, the shaper role was identified by all participants as existing within their organizations, if only informally. The role was not necessarily recognized by that name, but all participants stated that it was typical that someone would champion and 'shape' the project as it moved through the process from idea to initiation. The role is performed at a number of levels, whether by a sponsor, a project manager or a subject matter expert. The role can also be fulfilled by more than one person. The role itself, however, is not one that typically exists within the organizational hierarchy. It is described as being a responsibility that is taken on by someone who is working to get something done, who sees the need for a project to be initiated: 'It is typically the role that I play. I hesitate in terms of [using the word] "champion". In owning the assembly of resources and processes, yes, but I am engaging others that are the real champions and business owners of them' (10). Not only is the role of project shaper often not recognized in the structure of organizations, but a number of participants identified the role as one that is informal in nature: 'It is a typical role, but not an official one. Technically it is supposed to be the executive champion or business sponsor' (6). Given the informal nature of the role, it can be inferred that there are challenges in its execution; in particular, it may be difficult to understand the skills and strategies by which project shaping can be accomplished.

Table 8.1 illustrates the degree to which the categories that emerged in the current study align with the conceptual model proposed by Smith & Winter.

Table 8.1   Comparison of study categories with elements in
            Smith & Winter (2010)

Category details	Categories (current study)	Elements (Smith & Winter, 2010)	Element details
• Influence on the initiation process • Drivers of influence • Other roles with influence	Ability to influence	Shaper's volition	• Personal influence in the project • Ability and willingness to act
• Recognition of decision • Influence of politics • Facilitation of decision process	Agreement to initiate	Tribal power	• Recognition of multiple perspectives of the project • Social facilitation and negotiation
• Process consistency and formality • Formality of documentation • Effectiveness of process	Approach formality	Control model of projects	• Introduction of process • Establishment of appropriate controls
• Alignment with organizational priorities • Clarity of direction	Decision clarity	External dynamics – 'peripety'	• Recognition of external forces • Managing dynamics of change
• Information produced to support the decision process	Decision information	Enacted reality	• Creation of concrete evidence of the project
• Value of the proposed result	Decision value	Transformation and value	• Delivery of an effective solution • Creation of value for stakeholders
• Agency within the rule system • Clarity, formality and consistency of the rules • Explicit versus implicit emphasis of rules • Effectiveness of the rule system	Overall rule environment		

A comparison of the categories defined within the current study demonstrates that, while not perfectly aligned, there is a clear correlation between them and the elements defined by Smith & Winter. The predominant themes that have emerged from the participants in discussing the process of project initiation broadly intersect with the earlier conceptual framework of the project shaper. In addition to reinforcing the overall idea that a role of project shaper does exist, this also suggests that the initial conceptual development by Smith & Winter is still relevant when we are discussing a larger sample of participants than the three represented in their case studies. However, there is no direct correlation of terminology, nor is there an attempt to enforce one; the categories in the current study are ones that have emerged from the participant cases, and – in keeping with the principles of grounded theory – every effort has been maintained to align the terminology used with the concepts the participants themselves identified. Also, the concepts themselves do not align directly. In part, that is a question of focus; the narratives provided by Smith & Winter concern project managers responsible for not just the 'shaping', but also the delivery of the resulting project, whereas the current study very specifically looked only at the process of project initiation that led to an initiation decision, and did not for the most part consider subsequent planning and project management. In addition, Smith & Winter did not explore the role of rule systems in the decision making process. The current study creates a new category of analysis in its exploration of rule systems. This study adds the role of agency, which could in part be included in Smith & Winter's concept of 'actors' volition' and which appears here as a dimension of the understanding of the rules associated with initiation decisions. Overall, however, the results appear to provide support for reinforcing and validating the conceptual offering of Smith & Winter.

One key aspect in particular that emerges from the current study that did not appear in the discussion by Smith & Winter is the role of rules in the project initiation process. This dimension, which I introduced directly into the data collection process as an area of exploration as a result of insights I gained during the literature review, is one that was sustained and expanded during the data collection process. Not only did participants recognize the presence and operative role of implicit and explicit rules in how projects were initiated, they also frequently highlighted these as being different than the espoused processes they had previously been discussing. The idea of 'rules' is a concept I expanded considerably in later interviews, and the concept emerged as a major dimension of analysis in the current study. What this suggests is that while the conceptual elements Smith & Winter identified are important, these elements are operationalized and emphasized (or constrained) by an organization's overall rule environment.

Building on the discussion of agency, there is a need for actors to assess and evaluate the degree to which the role of project shaper exists in the organization. As has been noted, this might be a formal role or an informal one. Where it is formal, there will be established guidelines and expectations that form part of the larger framework of rules about how projects get initiated. Where the role is informal, there is much more potential latitude for movement and flexibility shaping a project, but also much more challenge and effort are required on the part of the individual playing the project shaper. In all instances, there is a need to integrate and navigate across the organizational expectations and the individual requirements of the project in order to arrive at an appropriate strategy the actor can actualize in shaping the project and supporting an effective initiation decision.

Practical Guidance for Shaping Projects

Putting together the insights and observations discussed above and the observations outlined in this section, what should those who find themselves needing – or expected – to support the initiation of a project do? How can they make informed and reasonable decisions about how to approach their role? What do they need to understand about the organization and other participants in order to support and guide making effective project initiation decisions? The following sections summarize the practical insights that have been realized in conducting the research discussed in this book. They provide concrete guidance for those who find themselves in the project shaper role, and suggestions about the practices that are most effective depending upon the culture, structure and values of the organization.

UNDERSTAND THE ORGANIZATION

Understanding the organization is about recognizing the environment and culture, and its influence on how project initiation decisions are made. In particular, there is a need to understand whether the organization is primarily process-driven or politically focused in how project initiation decisions are made. The mere presence of a defined process is not sufficient to address this question; a larger issue is whether or not the process is actually adhered to in supporting initiation decisions.

For organizations that are process-driven, there is a need to assess the formality and consistency in using the process. If the process is formal and consistently adhered to, then this is going to guide the rest of the initiation process.

High levels of formality and consistency are not common, but where they do exist, they provide clear expectations for how initiation decisions will occur, and constrain opportunities for individual autonomy. Also, understanding the clarity of how project initiation decisions is made is critical. Having a level of clarity about the process and criteria of making initiation decisions has a strong influence on decision making effectiveness, while arbitrary or unclear decision making approaches will compromise decision making effectiveness and again place a greater degree of emphasis on the individual playing the project shaper role.

For organizations that are politically focused, the implicit rule systems and cultural conventions of how things happen within the organization have a much stronger emphasis on initiation decisions. In these environments, the requirement is less one of process than it is of consensus and broad agreement, or the exercise of positional power. However, the key organizational influence in politically driven environments is how functional and constructive the politics of the organization actually is. Constructive environments that value collaboration, discussion and consensus are much more amenable to supporting effective decision making, while dysfunctional and hostile political environments make for a considerably larger challenge.

CLARIFY THE ROLE

In addition to taking stock of the organizational dynamics and rule systems, it is important to understand the clarity and expectations of the project shaper role. In highly process-driven organizations, this will be formally defined, as will the expectations and accountabilities of whoever serves as the project shaper. In politically driven organizations, there will often be much less role clarity and a greater need for individual adaptation within the role. The most important challenge is appreciating when the role is an informal one that is not clearly recognized within the organization. Informal definition of the role will place a much greater emphasis on the actions of the person assuming the role to secure support and ensure buy-in to a project initiation decision.

DETERMINE DECISION MAKING PRACTICES

For any project initiation decision, it is important to understand how the ultimate decision to proceed will be made, and by whom. As discussed above, those organizations that have a formal process will be more likely to have clear and specific guidelines on the process, criteria and decision making participants. In the absence of a formally defined process, this will require some exploration of how initiation decisions are typically arrived at and the influences that drive the decision making process. Particularly in more politically driven organizations, this may be more subjective and inconsistent. There may need to be some up-front negotiation regarding decision making expectations on an individual project basis. The challenge is to establish some clarity about who will be involved, what they are looking for and the expectations that need to be met for an initiation decision to be made.

ASSESS THE CAPACITY TO EXERCISE AGENCY

An essential issue for anyone in the project shaper role is understanding the degree to which there is capacity to exercise agency. As noted above, this can be constrained in contexts where there is strong process, or in environments dominated by dysfunctional politics and an informal shaper role. Beyond these two polarities, there is fairly broad space for free play on the part of the actors to exercise agency. Their ability to do so will still require both an assessment of organizational constraints, as discussed earlier, and the personal willingness to exercise independence and autonomy in service to the project being initiated.

EVALUATE THE PROJECT

How – and when – to exercise agency will in part depend upon the project and the degree to which there is already support and commitment to proceed with the project. Where the project strongly supports defined project criteria or there is a broad level of political support, less influence will be required in getting a project initiated. Where there is less support or commitment, the role of the project shaper will be that much more challenging, and there is a greater likelihood that some level of autonomy and influence will be required. It will be important to clearly evaluate and identify the merits of the project, the degree that these can be leveraged to obtain organizational and political support, and the actions that will be required to secure commitment to move forward with the project.

DEVELOP A STRATEGY

Each project requires a clear sense of what needs to be done to support its initiation. In particular, this requires a candid assessment of whether – and how – the project supports the objectives and priorities of the organization, and what will be required to secure commitment for the project to proceed. Individual project shapers need to consider what can be done to leverage the resources of the organization, and their own personal credibility and influence, to support realizing an effective decision. It is also important to recognize that an effective decision is not always one where the project is approved. A decision to defer or not proceed with a project can be just as relevant and appropriate, depending upon what is truly important for the organization.

Developing a strategy requires first understanding how organizational processes and supports can be leveraged. As discussed earlier, it requires an assessment of the processes, political environment and decision processes that influence how initiation decisions are made. It also requires an appreciation of how projects are ultimately initiated, and the degree to which these decisions are the product of a consistent and well-understood approach. It is important to understand the formality and recognition of the project shaper role, and the degree to which those who perform this role are recognized and supported within the organization. Finally, an assessment of the political support and availability of resources to guide, influence or inform the decision making process is critical.

On a personal level, project shapers need to take stock of their own ability to support the project initiation process. This includes understanding the influence they have in the decision making process, and the visibility and support available to them – or not – as a result of their position within the organization. In addition, they need to be conscious of the influences that best support establishing and reinforcing their credibility as shapers of the project. In process-based environments, credibility, due diligence and experience tend to be more strongly valued. Decision makers in these instances are looking to ensure that research has been done, that the recommendation is well thought out, and that those presenting the information have a mastery of the details behind the project. In politically driven organizations, there is more of an emphasis on communication, negotiation, proactive engagement and the exercise of political savvy. The focus in these instances is more on building consensus and buy-in politically than rationally selling the merits of the project.

COMMIT TO PERFORMING THE ROLE

Finally, project shapers need to commit to their role. Where those in the project shaper role are successful, it is in part because they have responsibly exercised their influence in supporting an effective decision being made. This requires confidence, commitment and purposeful action. Project shapers need to be comfortable that they have a role to play, that they have permission – or are willing to take independent action – to play that role, and to garner the political support and process credibility necessary to arrive at an effective decision.

This is where responsible exercising of agency is critical. It is not about exercising influence to support personal goals and ambitions; it is about ensuring that the project being championed is evaluated and considered in the best possible light with respect to the goals and priorities of the organization.

Conclusions

The exercise of agency is difficult, and requires a great deal of work and effort on the part of individuals performing the project shaper role. It is not just about working within the rules and guidelines of the organization, except in those rare circumstances where there is a formally defined and consistently adhered to process of project initiation. It requires a significant expenditure of personal effort in understanding the organization, evaluating and making a credible case for the individual project. It also requires investing personal commitment and political capital in lobbying, negotiating, consulting and shaping the project into something that makes the most sense for the organization. As has been discussed, the project shaper role exists in virtually every organization. However, what is necessary to perform that role varies considerably depending upon the culture, politics and processes at work within the organization. Effectiveness in the project shaper role certainly leverages the strengths and abilities of the individual actor, but success requires responsibly adapting personal qualities to what is necessary to secure organizational commitment and buy-in. This means that project shapers must intelligently and appropriately adapt their approach to the circumstances of the organization if they are to succeed in securing an effective initiation decision.

Chapter 9
Making Better Project Decisions

Introduction

Much of this book has so far focused on the role of the project shaper and the influence of personal agency in contributing to the development of effective project initiation decisions. Those who play the project shaper role fall into a variety of organizational categories. The role may be formal or informal in nature, depending in part upon how clearly defined the process of project initiation is within the organization. The project shaper may be the executive champion responsible for a project, a project manager or a subject matter expert. The level of influence can vary based upon positional authority, political influence or process expertise. In the majority of instances discussed thus far, however, the assumed audience for this book has been those in the project shaper role, and the focus has been on providing them with meaningful and useful guidance. The emphasis has largely been on empowering project shapers, regardless of their organizational position and influence, to perform their role effectively.

In this chapter, the focus shifts to the executive responsible for making the project initiation decisions. To the extent that the project shaper is the individual who champions and shapes organizational perceptions of the project being considered, the decision making executive is the person whose perceptions are being most directly shaped. Just the actors in the project shaper role need to exercise their role responsibly, so too must the executives making the ultimate decisions to proceed. To do so, it is important to understand the initiation process, and the influence that they have as decision makers on positively or negatively influencing the process environment in which this occurs, and its overall effectiveness. For the executive who is responsible for evaluating projects and making actual decisions on whether or not to proceed, this chapter provides insight into the influences at play, the processes at work and the means by which projects are presented. The intent is to provide guidance on what to look out for, what to avoid, and what questions to ask to make sure that you are making the best decision possible.

Influences that Shape How Project Information is Presented

When evaluating how project initiation decisions are made, and how project information is presented, a key differentiation is the fact that there are two roles that are operative in most initiation decisions: the project shaper and the project approver. One is responsible for developing, supporting, advocating for and championing the idea of the project within the organization; the other actually makes the decision to proceed with a proposed project. The key thing to recognize here is that these are *roles*: in some organizations, they are undertaken by the same person; in others, they represent two different individuals; in still others, the championing role may be diffuse, and in many others, the initiation decision may be undertaken by a team rather than an individual. Regardless, there are two essential roles that need to be understood and distinguished: that of project shaper and that of project approver.

The role of project shaper is one of advocate, however that may be actually exercised in the organization. In the stories of the individual research participants, the role most described was one of champion of a project idea. While the power and influence of the project shaper may vary, and in different organizational contexts can be formal or informal, it is present to some degree in all organizational contexts. For some organizations, it represents a role of champion leading from an executive level; other organizations see this as being the purview of the project manager; still others perceive it as being the responsibility of a subject matter expert with more detailed analytical knowledge of the initiative. In all instances, this is the role that presents and promotes the project to the organization. As the initiative transitions from an idea to an approved project, the project shaper role helps to support, encourage and champion its adoption by the organization.

The project approver is the role that ultimately makes the decision to proceed with a project. As noted above, this can be the role of an individual executive or an executive committee. The responsibility of this role is to evaluate the project against the overall priorities and strategic imperatives of the organization, and to determine whether or not it a project that should be undertaken. This is not a role of championing; it is a role of evaluation and decision. Based upon the strategic direction, objectives and organizational priorities of the organization, this role is responsible for determining whether or not to proceed with a specific project. Project approvers are the recipients of the analytical work associated with assessing and evaluating a project. They ultimately make the decision about whether or not to proceed with a particular project proposal.

Understanding the Influences at Play

In order to ensure an appropriate initiation process is in place, it is necessary to understand the influences that are operative in making project initiation decisions. The roles being undertaken will certainly have an impact, and all organizations in the research to date have indicated the presence of the project shaper role, as well as the presence of an approval role. Both of these roles vary in their formality, the rigour with which they are conducted and the level of the organization at which they exist. The most significant variation in both roles, however, is a product of the organizational processes and political dynamics by which they are managed. While project shapers must largely adapt to the forces that are present, executives within an organization in part have a role in shaping those forces. As the executive responsive for ultimately making – or guiding – the initiation decision, it is essential not just to understand which dynamics are at work, but also to recognize how those in the role shape and contribute to the creation of these dynamics.

PROCESS INFLUENCES

The processes supporting project initiation are inherent to the organization. As we have seen, however, the degree to which these are formally defined and consistently applied varies considerably, and have a significant impact on overall decision making effectiveness. Few organizations actually have a formally defined, consistently adhered to process of project initiation. Where decision making effectiveness is highest, however, is in those rare circumstances where there are high levels of process formality and consistency. This produces a uniform environment of decision making, where expectations are clear and are universally adhered to. But it is equally important to recognize that where the process is more formal and consistent, this also constrains opportunities for individual flexibility and autonomy. Organizations that desire consistency and formality primarily do so in order to ensure that all projects are objectively and impartially reviewed; the emphasis is on the process producing good results, rather than focusing on the merits of any individual project. This is a unique environment, and as already noted, it is not a common one. Few organizations are actually willing to accept and work within the narrow constraints that truly rigorous and consistently adhered to process creates.

If there is a desire for more formality, it is important to be clear about both the expectations and consequences of increasing the formality and consistency of project initiation decisions. Not only is the degree of agency and influence of the project shaper constrained in strongly driven process environments, but the decision making process itself is much more rigorous and defined. For organizations that adopt such an approach, there is a stated and desired value of ensuring process adherence, demanding complete objectivity and clearly articulating expectations and decision criteria in advance. The other consequence, of course, is that there is far less room within the process for discretion, judgement and flexibility. This has to be appropriate for the culture of the organization, and there has to be a willingness to commit to – and ensure – adherence. Where there is no intent to embrace this level of adherence, going through the motions often does more harm than good. Where actions and stated intent do not align, this will be apprehended quickly by actors within the organization. The message received is that the organization does not walk its talk, is not serious about process adherence, and that the process can be – and is intended to be – subverted.

The other process-related factor that influences project initiation decisions is the clarity of the decision making process itself. To a certain extent, this is a hygiene factor, in that the impact occurs when the decision making process is not clear. Where there is a lack of clarity about the decision making process – including both how the decision will be made and the criteria to be employed – there is a significantly greater degree of challenge in supporting individual projects and in generally navigating the organizational environment. Even where the decision making process for a single project must be unique, whether because of size or complexity, executives can help to support the effectiveness of the process by setting clear expectations about how the decision will be made, who will be involved in making the decision, and the criteria that will be employed.

POLITICAL INFLUENCES

Many more organizations make project initiation decisions as a result of political influences than do so using a formal and consistent process. In fact, where processes exist that are not formally defined or consistently adhered to, project initiation decisions are also often more influenced by politics than they are by what process is in place. The political environment strongly shapes the decision making approach within organizations, and executives responsible for making initiation decisions are well advised to maintain awareness of the political environment – and their own influence in shaping this environment. With respect to project initiation decisions, the research reported here has identified that decision effectiveness in political environments is primarily influenced by two factors: the dysfunctionality of politics within the organization, and the approach project shapers adopt in approaching their role.

Dysfunctional politics – or the absence of constructive politics – will likely be firmly entrenched. Bringing about change in the political environment is long, involved and requires significant effort, and is beyond the scope of what can reasonably be discussed here. Nevertheless, the influence of dysfunctional or ineffective politics is significant, and has been demonstrated to significantly undermine decision making effectiveness. While wholesale change may be out of the question, there is still the opportunity for decision makers to consider how politics is influencing the presentation and evaluation of an individual project decision. From here, the executive may have some – or significant – latitude to confront, challenge or offset the influence of politics. This might be through the declaration of specific principles that will guide this particular decision, the highlighting of conspicuously political positions or perspectives, or setting explicit guidelines and expectations for how the decision at hand will be managed. This does not prevent the exercising of politics, of course, and it does not preclude the attempt to exercise influence by others, but in isolated instances, it can help to create a greater level of objectivity and transparency, should that be appropriate and desired.

The other predominant influence on decision making effectiveness is in how the role of the project shaper is exercised. While part of this is a product of how individuals approach the role, a fundamental organizational consideration is the degree to which the role is formally recognized and established. To some degree, this is again a hygiene factor, in that it is the absence of project shaper formality that influences decision making effectiveness. Where the role is informal, decision making is much more likely to be ineffective. Project approving executives again have some influence on this, from two different perspectives. First, they can help to ensure recognition and formalization of the role, even if only in the context of a specific project decision. Secondly, they are able to exercise influence based upon who is assigned and selected to perform the project shaper role, and the expectations created and communicated in making the appointment.

As has been identified throughout this book, the individuals playing the project shaper role – and the degree of agency they exercise within the role – have a critical influence on decision making effectiveness. This last influence is also political, but it is the exercise of personal political power and influence by the individual who assumes the role of project shaper. Project approving executives need to be aware of the potential and likelihood of agency being exercised, however, as well as the degree to which they can help to promote – or inhibit – the exercising of agency in performing their role. This is discussed in more detail in the next section.

INDIVIDUAL INFLUENCES

The most significant influence on decision making effectiveness within this research has been the degree of agency exercised by someone performing the project shaper role. For the approving executive, it is helpful to understand where and how this influence is exercised, and the impact it has on how decisions are made. It is also valuable to understand how opportunities for exercising agency can be influenced by the approving executive. This influence occurs in a number of ways, and can be overt or subtle. It begins with the selection of who will be assigned to the project shaper role, the expectations and guidelines that are communicated to them, and the degree of support and assistance that is afforded to them during the project initiation process.

Selection of the project shaper is significant. As discussed above, the degree of agency exercised by project shapers is primarily a product of position within the organization, decision making influence and personality. Identifying a project shaper who is higher up in the organization chart, and has a strong degree of experience and credibility, will therefore create an opportunity for the actor in that role to exercise a greater degree of agency. Having a voice in the decision making process also has a positive influence, and while this section presumes a separation between the roles of project shaper and project approver, this is not always the case; they may, in some instances, be the same person. Even where the roles are separated, this does not mean that project shapers cannot have a voice in the process and a role in the decision. Ensuring that their involvement is more than passive, and includes the allowance for input into the decision making process, or the articulation of a recommendation, again allows latitude for greater levels of agency to be asserted. Finally, the personality of the project shaper is a consideration. Someone who is confident, goal-oriented, enthusiastic and purposeful is most likely to willingly exercise agency in their role of shaping the project opportunity and influencing the subsequent initiation decision.

Of course, the converse is also true. Selecting a project shaper who is not senior in the organization is more likely to result in less willingness and perceived ability to exercise agency. Constraining input and involvement in the decision making process will equally constrain the exercise of agency. And selecting someone who is more sensitive to organizational norms, cautious, risk-averse and sensitive to the expectations of others is far less likely to result in the autonomous and independent behaviour associated with agency.

In addition to who is selected for the role, the approving executive can shape the degree to which the project shaper will exercise agency through the expectations that are articulated in assigning the role. Identifying that there is a desire in evaluating a project to challenge conventional thinking, to pursue innovation, and for the project to be a source of significant change will reinforce the need for the project shaper to challenge norms and conventions. Reinforcing the need for caution, consensus and maintenance of the status quo, or the need for caution in engaging politically with stakeholders, will likely have a restraining influence on the exercise of agency.

Finally, the manner in which expectations are set with the rest of the organization regarding the project opportunity, the initiation process and the role of the project shaper in guiding that process will create opportunities to allow – or inhibit – agency. The degree to which the initiative is seen as important or critical, the extent to which change is required or advocated for, and the level of political support and visibility afforded by the approving executive will all influence the ability to exercise agency. Where the project shaper is seen as a champion for the project, acting with the trust and support of the approving executive or senior management team, the corresponding authority and delegated power will encourage an environment that permits a greater degree of agency. Lack of visible support or commitment, by contrast, will serve to undermine the influence and agency of the project shaper.

The Influences of How Projects are Presented

A separate but significant consideration for the approving executive is how decisions are presented, and the influences – often unconscious – that can fundamentally bias the decision making process. These influences draw on the essential principles of behavioural decision making discussed in the Introduction to this book. They represent important considerations decision makers should keep in mind as they evaluate and consider projects being presented for initiation. These cautions are not unique to the process of project initiation, but are relevant for any decision. Nor are they easy to dispel or overcome. Daniel Kahneman, the Nobel Prize-winning economist who developed prospect theory in collaboration with Amos Tversky, offered this observation: 'We documented systematic errors in the thinking of normal people, and we traced these errors to the design of the machinery of cognition rather than to the corruption of thought by emotion' (Kahneman, 2011, p. 8).

The essentials of prospect theory in particular offer important insights and cautions to decision makers. An essential tenet of prospect theory is that we set a reference point, from which we judge the relative advantages or disadvantages of a particular choice. This is often, but not always, the status quo, the implication being that we evaluate a decision based upon how much better or worse its outcomes will be based upon our current position. The challenge is that we adjust our reference point quite quickly, where even very recent gains are assimilated and form our frame of reference. Prospect theory also reinforces our aversion to losses; we avoid putting ourselves in situations where we will be less well off than we are today. This makes us risk-averse, in that we lock in gains and are cautious about putting them at risk in the future. The challenge is that our preferences do not hold true in the face of losses; where performance declines from our reference point, we actually become more prone to take on risks. The consequences of these facts for project initiation decisions is interesting, and influenced primarily by how project opportunities are presented. Where the promised consequences of a project are presented as potential gains, decision makers tend to be more cautious, and will pursue safer strategies that avoid high-risk propositions. When exactly the same opportunities are framed as potential losses, however, decision makers tend to select riskier options and pursue higher-risk strategies.

What is important to note is that, as decision makers, we will do this in making decisions about exactly the same choice, depending upon how the problem and proposed solution are framed. Consider an example where an organizational change project is being proposed that will impact a 500-person division. Framing the consequences as 'saving 300 jobs' will inspire cautious behaviour, while framing the consequences as '200 people will lose their job' will promote the acceptance of greater risk on the part of decision makers. The outcomes are the same; the difference is only in how the choices have been described.

The concept of anchoring also has a significant influence on decision making. The idea is simple, but one that has profound consequences. Our minds, having heard a number, will 'anchor' on that and judge subsequent estimates as greater or less based upon that first number. This is the phenomenon at play where projects, once an initial estimate is communicated, tend to be saddled with that estimate, regardless of the degree of thought or rigour that went into its development. We are also prone to anchoring when we go into a restaurant; read the menu, and you will be struck by the price of the most expensive entrée. The restaurant knows that some people will order it, for the prestige of ordering the most expensive thing on the menu. For the rest of us, however, it serves a slightly more insidious role: it provides an anchor point that makes the prices of the remaining entrées seem more reasonable. We can be manipulated in terms of the order in which options are presented as well. If I present three potential options within a business case, starting with the more expensive option establishes a ceiling below which other options appear more reasonable. Starting with the least expensive option, however, instils greater resistance to the consideration of higher-priced options.

Decision makers are also influenced by representativeness and availability, which reference distinct but related concepts concerning how likely we consider an event based upon stereotypical similarities, and how familiar and accessible we find options related to the question under consideration. For example, we will be more amenable to a solution that addresses problems we are familiar with and can readily relate to. We will also be more open to solutions that are in line with our expectations and are similar to examples we are already familiar with. The harder it is to think of examples of a situation or problem, the more likely we are to diminish its likelihood of occurring, and the more unfamiliar a solution, the less likely we are to be drawn to it.

One of the most fundamental influences that affects both decision makers and project shapers alike, however, is confirmation bias. Confirmation bias influences our decision making in that we tend to look for information that reflects our beliefs, and to discount information that does not conform. This is particularly pernicious when we are confronted with ambiguous information; rather than recognizing that the information could be interpreted in multiple ways, and in turn prompting us that we need to seek additional insight to establish the correct interpretation, we default to interpreting the ambiguity in a way that supports our position. The result is that we look for information that confirms our beliefs and supports our hypotheses, and tend to discount, ignore and discredit contrary evidence.

As mentioned above, these decision making biases are innate and fundamental to all of us. They are operating daily, and influence the decisions we make regularly – whether large or small. Making effective decisions therefore means that we need to develop strategies that consciously force us to confront our biases and consider options from multiple angles. For the approving executive evaluating whether to initiate a project, this means considering the benefits and the consequences of an initiation decision. It means consciously evaluating projects from all sides, and deliberately seeking disconfirming and contrary opinions. We need to consider expert advice, particularly where projects address aspects that may be only tangential to our areas of experience, and seek objective data regarding the actual probability and impact of potential outcomes. In particular, we need to objectively and honestly assess the actual costs and the realistic benefits of projects. We need to evaluate the merits of what can be objectively known and understood, regardless of previous estimates, and beware that there is a fundamental tendency – built into how we think about and sell projects – to underplay the costs and overemphasize the potential benefits.

Making Better Decisions

This chapter focuses on how to help executives responsible for project initiation decisions to perform their role more effectively. We have explored how the role of the approving executive differs from – but is supported by – the project shaper. We have discussed the influences of different decision making environments from the perspective of the approving executive, and discussed what to consider regarding the environment as well as the importance of recognizing the influence executives themselves have in creating the environment. Finally, we have discussed the unconscious – but very real – biases that exist in how decisions are made, and the factors that need to be evaluated and considered in order to respond to these biases appropriately. That represents a lot of information, and a number of different perspectives. And as was made clear in Chapter 1, decision makers only have so much attention and so much cognitive attention. To simplify and summarize, the following points outline practical guidelines for the approving executive in making effective project initiation decisions. It outlines what to look for, questions to ask and what situations to avoid, whether you are considering one project or an entire business plan full of opportunities.

WHAT TO LOOK FOR

In making a project initiation decision, the key considerations are that there is an actual problem, a viable solution, broad support and consideration of the implications necessary to implement the solution and have it adopted by its target organization. For the approving executive, the following would be an appropriate checklist to consider in evaluating whether a project is ready to proceed:

- **Confidence** – Is the champion of the project confident about the solution they are presenting? Do they have a level of mastery in terms of the problem, the solution and its implications for the business?

As one of the research participants indicated, this is a key measure for many executives: 'The executive wants and is comfortable with a statement that is provided with "moral confidence", that has clear expertise. That is not just whim. The ability of the person to be able to understand the details, where if they press, they will get a solid answer back' (6). This is a key measure of not just the effectiveness of the project shaper in their role, but the degree to which the work has been done to evaluate the project opportunity effectively.

- **Comprehensiveness** – Does what is being presented for approval cover all the bases in terms of what needs to be understood to make an initiation decision? This is not to confuse detail and number of pages with quality of analysis. Done well, a comprehensive answer may be presented in just a few pages or slides. Comprehensiveness is a measure of demonstrating that the thinking that went into the answer is appropriate, thorough, and leads to an appropriate and relevant conclusion.

- **Consultation** – As well having done the work, has the necessary consultation occurred with other stakeholders? Has there been sufficient assessment of the problem the project would solve and why it is a problem for those who are impacted? Is there broad agreement on the proposed solution and its relevance? Is there commitment and willingness amongst stakeholders to accept the proposed solution, to commit to the identified benefits and to work to ensure that they are realized? Are stakeholders committed to the solution, and what it means for them within their roles?

Overall, the above points focus on testing that what is being proposed as a solution is meaningful and relevant, that an appropriate level of investigation of problems and possible solutions has occurred, and that stakeholders who will be impacted by (and expected to adopt and use) the results of the project understand what the proposed project means to them, value the solution and are committed to delivering value from that solution. Answering these questions is also a test of how well the project shaper has performed their role in developing, championing and proposing the project to the organization.

QUESTIONS TO ASK

Focusing on the solution itself, there are a number of questions approving executives need to consider to satisfy themselves as to whether or not the proposal is reasonable, and that they can be reasonably comfortable moving forward with the initiative:

- **Who has been involved?** – Really, this question is derived from the exploration of stakeholder commitment. It addresses two fundamental issues that otherwise often compromise the initiation of projects: have all of the right stakeholders been consulted, and are those stakeholders committed to implementing the results and realizing value? In other words, when an initiation decision is made, is there broad support for proceeding with that project? While this sounds like a question that is more relevant for politically driven organizations, it is equally relevant where process drives the decision process. Selection and implementation still depend upon people, and those stakeholders still need to care about and value the outcome for the project to make sense and for the results to be supported.

- **What assumptions were made?** –In all projects being proposed, it is important to recognize that assumptions (and a significant number of them) will have been made to shape the proposal to the extent that it is ready to be presented. These will include assumptions about what is important to the organization, what compromises are reasonable, and what activities will be required to complete the project and implement the results. Assumptions will be made about the resources required during the project, the timelines necessary to do the work, and the costs that comprise both the estimated costs and the projected benefits. Understanding the assumptions that have been made is critical to evaluating a proposed project. The focus of approving executives should be on evaluating whether or not they agree with the assumptions. If the assumptions are well grounded, they should establish a strong foundation to evaluate the rest of the proposal. Where the assumptions are questionable, they may need to be revised and the impacts of changes to these assumptions will need to be assessed.

- **What options were considered?** – By the time a project is proposed, the options associated with a proposed solution have often been whittled down to a select few. In fact, it may be that only one option is being presented. For the approving executive, the important thing to understand is how the proposed solutions were arrived at. What were the thinking processes, and what decisions led to the selection of the options that were proposed? This is in part a test of the potential biases of the project shaper and the team doing the analysis, in that they may have been drawn towards specific choices to the exclusion of others. It is also a question that can provide important insights into how the possible biases of the approving executive are perceived by others.

- **What choices were dismissed early on?** – Understanding the potential solutions that were eliminated early in the process can provide some key insights into the thinking that went into the analysis, and the real assumptions that underlie the project being proposed. Options that are not analysed in detail tend to be ignored because they do not meet some fundamental criteria. It is these criteria that can sometimes best articulate the perceived constraints and the perceived objective of a project. Understanding these criteria therefore provides an important lens through which to interpret and evaluate what is being proposed.

- **What are the risks?** – Risk is an essential consideration in evaluating any project proposal. For the approving executive, there is a need to consider risk from a number of perspectives. First, there needs to be a level of comfort that an appropriate level of risk analysis has been done, simply as a test of the analytical work that led into the project proposal being developed. Secondly, and more importantly, there needs to be agreement on what the risks are, and the analysis of the probabilities and impacts associated with the risks that have been identified. Finally, and most critically, there needs to be an appreciation for the organization's appetite for risk, and the degree to which the proposed risk response strategies align with that appetite. In other words, as an approving executive, are you comfortable with the risks that have been outlined? Do you accept the proposed strategies? And are you willing to deal with the fact that whatever has been defined may actually play out?

- **How realistic are the costs?** – This is obviously an important question for any approving executive. Apart from knowing the number that represents the cost estimate, there is a need to understand the reasonability of that cost estimate. There is a tendency, again because of our psychological biases (and to create favourable conditions by which the project is evaluated), to downplay costs and presume against risk. To counter this, approving executives need to be comfortable not just with the cost numbers being presented, but also with how those estimates were developed. A couple of key questions to consider in assessing the costs are: How sensitive are they to increases? What would cause them to increase?

- **How realistic are the benefits?** – Alongside the costs of any project proposal, there should be an understanding of the benefits. As with costs, there is a very real and very human tendency to be unrealistic in assessing benefits. Unlike costs, however, the tendency with benefits is to overplay and exaggerate them. In other words, benefits tend to be inflated over and above what is realistically possible, once again in order to make the project as attractive as possible. And again, much of this manipulation may not be conscious; it often draws on our unconscious biases and inherent sense of optimism. As with costs, therefore, raising questions to assess the sensitivity and realism of the benefits is important. In particular, the approving executive should understand how sensitive the benefits are to not being attained. In addition to understanding these drivers, an important follow-on exploration is an assessment of what factors would cause the benefits to decrease.

- **Am I comfortable moving forwards?** – This is a difficult question to answer, because it relates to the appetite for risk and relative agency of the approving executive. It is also, in reality, the question that most impedes making actual project initiation decisions. If you can positively answer all of the previous questions with a favourable result, then there is every likelihood that the approving executive should be comfortable with proceeding. If favourable answers have been attained and there is still discomfort, that raises some significant concerns that it is important to explore. What is keeping you from moving forward? What is nagging at your subconscious that makes you uncomfortable? It is important for all approving executives to recognize that, even with answers to the questions outlined above, they are still dealing with uncertainty. You can't predict the future, and you can't guarantee the outcomes of a project when you approve it (and particularly not as early as you are going to be called upon to make an approval decision). Being comfortable with ambiguity, clear about the priorities of the organization and objective about the degree to which a given project supports those priorities is the job of the approving executive. Those are the tests you need to look for in agreeing to proceed.

SITUATIONS TO AVOID

While the questions above are designed to test the thinking behind a project proposal and provide guidance to approving executives as they evaluate individual opportunities, there are a couple of final considerations that are critical in making a project initiation decision. Possibly most usefully and relevantly, they should also help to provide some assurance to executives that when they do decide to proceed with a project, they still have controls and safety valves in place. The following, based upon insights from the research as well as experiences in recovering from (and sometimes cancelling) failed projects, represent some final – but critical – considerations.

- **Scenarios of 'must proceed'** – It is inevitable in project initiation decisions that there is some level of rhetoric at play. Projects are sold. Project proposals will vouch for their importance, the value that will be delivered and the benefits that will accrue to the organization should an initiation decision be made. The challenge is when this rhetoric starts to get out of hand, and projects start being presented as 'essential', 'mission-critical' or 'do or die'. Without question, there are some times when projects are genuinely essential and the success or failure of the organization is in the balance. These situations should not be frequent, however, and when you are in one of these circumstances, the stakes should already be pretty clear. So spelling them out is largely a restatement of the obvious. The point here is that sponsoring executives need to be cautious of inflammatory, inflationary rhetoric that presents projects as critical to organizational survival. The organization is functioning today – maybe not optimally, but it is functioning. If you do not instigate the project, you will still be where you are right now. Maintaining a realistic perspective on the requirements for the project, the opportunities for success and the consequences of failure is absolutely critical in making an objective decision about whether or not the project should proceed.

- **Committing where significant uncertainties still exist** – Projects are, by their nature, uncertain. At the same time, some projects are more uncertain than others. The challenge for approving executives is to effectively and appropriately weigh the uncertainties that are present, and make an appropriate judgement about the viability of the project and whether or not to proceed. What is critical here is making an appropriate and judicious decision. If you cannot see all the way to the finish line with clarity, it is dangerous to commit yourself to reaching that finish line. This does not mean that you should not proceed; you may well need to make an approval decision in the face of remaining uncertainties. What it does mean is that you should only commit to proceed as far as is reasonable given the uncertainties that are present. In weighing approval decisions, consider making staged approvals to help the organization manage its uncertainties. Approve an initial piece of work that investigates or explores the options, or moves forward in clarifying what is currently unknown, with a commitment to re-evaluate and revisit that approval as more becomes known. This concept is similar to the concept of driving according to the speed of your headlights: in the dark, you only drive as fast as will allow you to stop safely within the distance you can see. Driving beyond the range of your headlights heralds untold additional risk; approving your project beyond your ability to see forward arguably does the same.

- **Proceeding without meaningful off-ramps** – Off-ramps for projects are critical. Often referred to as 'stage-gates', they represent key decision points at which to evaluate whether or not to proceed with the project. The key questions that need to be asked at each meaningful stage-gate are twofold: Am I comfortable that the project is proceeding well, and can deliver successfully on its commitments? And secondly, does the organization still value realizing the results from the project? The importance of having off-ramps is that, should the answer to either of those questions be 'no', the organization needs to consider fundamentally revising the project so that it is valued and can be successful, or it needs to consider cancelling the project altogether. Off-ramps are the mechanisms that lead to cancellation. They prompt the organization to weigh and evaluate its investment, and allow it to exit the investment if it is no longer projected to deliver a meaningful return. They also need to allow for severing any contractual commitments that may have been undertaken should the project itself no longer be viable.

Conclusions

Unlike the other chapters of this book, which have largely explored and emphasized the role of the project shaper, this chapter focused primarily on the role of the approving executive. As I mentioned at the outset, this is the role that is so often being shaped in evaluating and deciding to proceed forward with a project. Making effective project initiation decisions not only requires appropriate and responsible exercising of the project shaper role, it also requires meaningful and relevant execution of the role by the approving executive. I have tried to reinforce what the approving executive needs to understand about the environment of the organization, and about the role of the project shaper. I have also identified those aspects of the environment over which the approving executive has influence. In particular, approving executives play a role in influencing how project initiation decisions are shaped through how they select the person that will perform the project shaper role, the expectations they establish and the manner in which this role is communicated to the organization.

Making effective project initiation decisions also critically requires being aware of the information that is presented, and the unconscious biases that can influence the decision making process. This includes the biases of those who are preparing and presenting the information (and, in particular, the project shaper), as well as those who are receiving, interpreting and ultimately taking action – and making decisions – based upon that information. This leads to fundamental tests – and questions – that approval executives can ask to make sure that they understand the projects being proposed, are comfortable with the rigour and analysis to date, and are comfortable with the implications of making a decision. The most important consideration here, of course, is actually making a decision. It is at the point of choice that many decision making processes break down, and many decision makers fail to commit to a course of action. This commitment, of course, could be not to proceed, just as much as it could be a choice to move forward. But in all instances, it should be a firm choice – a decision made, expressed and resolved.

Chapter 10

Improving the Project
Initiation Process

Introduction

This book has focused on helping to understand how project initiation decisions are made, and exploring the influences that lead to more effective decisions. The emphasis has been on understanding the organization as it is, recognizing the cultural and organizational drivers at work, and working within the constraints of those drivers. Depending upon the role, and influence, of individuals – whether as project shapers or approving executives – they will have more or less impact in being able to evolve and change the organization. The evolution of organizational culture is a slow, involved, difficult and time-consuming process. In the face of any project initiation decision, the emphasis is therefore on ensuring that particular decision is as effective as possible, and on working within the boundaries of the organization as they exist at the time.

None the less, there are times when we recognize that the approach of the organization as a whole needs to shift. The focus then moves from evaluating the current constraints associated with a particular initiation decision to defining the desired approach for all initiation decisions. The cause of this change may be a dissatisfaction with the current approach, or a recognition that a different approach could be more effective. In all instances, it requires consciously considering what a more effective approach might look like, and the actions and influences necessary to bring that change about. This chapter focuses on helping to guide the overall improvement of project initiation decisions. It provides guidance on understanding the current practices, considering desired future capabilities, and supporting the shift to a new approach to making project initiation decisions.

Assessing How Decisions are Made Today

UNDERSTANDING CURRENT DIMENSIONS

As discussed earlier, the three key drivers of decision making effectiveness are the effectiveness of processes, the effectiveness of the politics or implicit rule system of the organization, and the agency of project shapers and individual decision makers. In choosing to consider an ideal decision making environment for the organization, it is necessary to first understand the influence these drivers have today, and the relevance and value of these same drivers in the desired future framework for how project initiation decisions will be made.

Where there is a desire to improve the overall decision making environment, it is helpful to assess the current state of the organization in terms of each of these dimensions, rather than simply focusing on one. The aim is to understand all of the influences that currently shape how project initiation decisions are made, and how those will influence the design of the future decision making process. In other words, there should be consideration of the degree to which process, politics and personal agency all influence how project initiation decisions are currently made.

It is also important to recognize that all of these factors may be operative to some degree at the same time. They may interact, or there may be more emphasis on one dimension or another for specific project types, whereas other dimensions may be more prevalent or have greater influence on other project types. Understanding the relative influence of each dimension, and how they interact – positively or negatively – will provide a full and complete picture of the current decision making environment.

EVALUATING CURRENT EFFECTIVENESS

In evaluating the effectiveness of each dimension of the decision making process, it is helpful to consider each of the influencing factors that have been identified and discussed, and how they currently contribute to the effectiveness of that dimension. The following bullet points provide a summary of the key questions to consider with respect to each dimension.

- **Process effectiveness** – The assessment of process effectiveness focuses on the degree to which process drives and enables effective project initiation decisions within the organization. This tests the degree to which the consideration and evaluation of project initiation decisions follows a documented, agreed upon and commonly understood process. Specific questions to be considered include:

- *Degree of formality* – Formality focuses on whether the process is documented, identifies expectations in sufficient detail, and provides a sufficient level of rigour to support the evaluation of project opportunities. There is a need to assess how well-defined and formally articulated a process is in place today, and the level of appropriateness and rigour of the process in supporting the evaluation of project opportunities.
- *Degree of consistency* – Consistency focuses on the extent to which the process is actually adhered to, and how closely the process is followed. While formality and consistency are related, they do not necessarily vary together. An informal process can still be applied consistently, and a formally defined process may exist as a documented reality, and yet not reflect what actually occurs in making project initiation decisions. The process may also exhibit and respond to variations that the process does not directly acknowledge.
- *Clarity* – Understanding the decision making process itself focuses on what occurs at the time of choosing whether or not to proceed with a project proposal. In particular, this explores how well it is understood how a decision will be made, who will be involved in making this decision, and the criteria that will be employed in determining whether to proceed. Of particular concern is whether the process is arbitrary and unclear.
- *Evaluating the credibility of the project shaper* – In particular in process-driven environments, this focuses on the degree to which credibility is established through the reputation, experience and track record of the project shaper, and the degree to which the project shaper reinforces and emphasizes a focus on due diligence and adherence to process in approaching their role.

- **Political/rule system effectiveness** – The assessment of political or rule system effectiveness focuses on the degree to which political influences and the implicit rule system of the organization influence and shape how project initiation decisions are arrived at. This tests the extent to which consensus and personal relationships influence project initiation choices, and how an understanding of the implicit rules of 'how things get done here' influence those involved in the initiation process. Specific questions to be considered include:

– *What is the political environment of the organization in making project initiation decisions?* – Understanding the political environment assesses the degree to which there is a collaborative and effective level of politics within the organization, particularly amongst those who are involved in ultimately making project initiation decisions. In particular, there is a need to understand the extent to which the political environment is constructive, characterized by decision making approaches that emphasize collaboration, consensus and negotiation. Alternatively, the political environment may be perceived as being obstructive or negative, where political behaviours are dysfunctional, ineffective or characterized by avoidance of conflict.

– *How formally defined is the project shaper role?* – Exploring the formality of the project shaper role emphasizes the degree to which it is formally articulated, recognized and valued within the organization. It explores the extent to which there is recognition and appreciation of the need to champion ideas as they evolve from opportunity to project and ensure they best meet the needs of the organization. Alternatively, the project shaper role may be informally recognized, with a corresponding lack of visibility, profile and consideration necessary to appropriately evaluate project opportunities.

– *How is the political credibility of the project shaper demonstrated?* – In particular, this explores the degree to which the project shaper in a political context leverages relationships, proactive communications and political savvy in championing and supporting the exploration of the project opportunity. There is also a need to consider the extent to which the project shaper leverages position and delegated authority in shaping the project opportunity.

• **Personal agency** – The assessment of personal agency evaluates the degree to which the autonomy, flexibility and personal efforts of the project shaper primarily drive the project initiation process. This evaluates the extent to which project initiation decisions are ultimately shaped and determined by the individual responsible for championing and shaping definition of the project opportunity and its presentation for consideration by the approving executive. Specific questions to be considered include:

– *What is the typical position of someone in the project shaper role?* – Of particular interest is the level of authority and relative power and influence of those who typically assume responsibility for shaping project opportunities. There is a need to understand the formal level of influence, power and status of those who serve as project shapers, and the corresponding degree of credibility and authority they enjoy in their role.

–   *What is the decision making involvement of someone in the project shaper role?* – In understanding the decision making influence, there is a need to establish how much of a voice the project shaper has once a proposed project reaches the point of making a decision about whether or not to proceed. In particular, there is a need to understand the extent to which the project shaper merely facilitates the development of the project proposal, makes a recommendation regarding a potential project, whether they have input into the decision making process or actually participate in the decision.

–   *How do those in the project shaper role approach their role?* – The earlier discussion of the project shaper role covered the influence of personality. While this is difficult to assess objectively, it is also less of an issue when evaluating the current effectiveness of the decision making process than is understanding the actual behaviours exhibited by those who are shaping project opportunities. Do project shapers exercise a strong level of autonomy and independence in defining, evaluating and presenting projects? Or is there a level of sensitivity, caution and risk-aversion in how project opportunities are explored and presented?

By evaluating the dimensions described above and considering the questions that have been posed, a comprehensive understanding of the current influences on project initiation decisions can be gained. In particular, there will be an appreciation of those influences that have emerged from the study discussed here that have the greatest degree of influence on decision making effectiveness. Based upon this assessment – regardless of the stated biases or presumptions of how the decision making process works – it will be possible to identify those influences that in reality have the greatest influence on how project initiation decisions are made. These insights help to understand how decisions work in practice, rather than in theory. They represent the basis of what must be understood in determining how to proceed in improving the process of decision making.

Evaluating How Decisions Should be Made

Defining how project initiation decisions should be made requires a shift in thinking. We are transitioning from describing the world as it is to contemplating the world as we desire it to be. We are shifting from an evaluation of the practices as they exist to an assessment of the practices as they ought to be.

Identifying how project initiation decisions need to be made in future requires consideration of three key perspectives:

1.   What are the values that govern how the organization wants to make project initiation decisions in future?

2.   How much of a departure is the desired future state from how decisions are currently made?

3.   How much commitment and willingness exists within the organization to move from the current state to the desired future state?

In contemplating this transition, it is important to recognize that all of the challenges normally associated with making significant levels of organizational change will be operative when considering a shift to the process of initiating projects. As discussed in Chapter 1, projects are often considered the means by which organizational strategy is implemented. They are themselves the source of considerable influence and change in how the organization operates. Deciding which projects to proceed with therefore has considerable impact on the organization, and is subject to extensive political influence. Control of the project initiation process in many respects represents control over the strategic agenda of the organization.

Given this reality, there will be those who strongly favour an approach that imposes a new order of managing the evaluation of project opportunities. There will also be those who are strongly opposed, and who perceive any change to be a threat to the status quo and their current influence over the process. In other words, there are some people that benefit from the decision making process as it currently exists. There are also those who are disadvantaged by the current process. Those who currently benefit are most likely to resist the change, and those who struggle are most likely to support it. The most important question to ask at this point is: *To what extent is there collective, broad willingness to change the process of how projects are initiated?*

Where there is a broad enough level of support, where a critical mass of stakeholders see the value of changing the initiation process, the probabilities of success can be considered to be reasonable. Where this level of support is absent, or where there is critical and influential opposition, the chances of success are commensurately lower. It is important to make a real, pragmatic and honest assessment of the likelihood of meaningful change to the process occurring.

It is also important to consider the values that are most important in making a change to the project initiation process, and what problems this is specifically intended to solve. A variety of challenges may currently be present. There may be issues with resource capacity and a sheer lack of availability of resources to get project work done, where a new process is needed to better make decisions about the magnitude of change the organization can reasonably implement and successfully deliver. There may be challenges with ensuring that initiatives are best aligned with the strategic priorities of the organization and deliver the greatest value. There may be problems associated with the objective evaluation of opportunities, and a need to improve the accuracy and enhance deliberations about the costs of initiatives and the relative benefits they will deliver. There may be a desire to reduce the political influence and increase the overall objectivity with which potential projects are being evaluated. And the organization may want to promote improved collaboration and greater establishment of consensus, buy-in and commitment in deciding which projects to undertake.

All of the aforementioned perspectives represent perfectly viable and meaningful reasons to consider enhancing the process of project initiation within an organization. Each explanation is a product of different challenges that are likely being experienced in how the organization operates. Resolution of each challenge, and attainment of each objective, emphasizes different values and principles. Most importantly, each value will be best supported by a different solution, and will require a different focus in endeavouring to improve the effectiveness of project initiation decisions.

As was observed in the study findings, what works most effectively depends upon what is most valued. The three greatest influences on decision effectiveness were the effectiveness of process, politics and individual actors in supporting the initiation of individual projects. Each of these dimensions can work, and can support the making of effective and appropriate decisions. The approach that is emphasized will depend upon the culture, structure and values of the organization. Where there is a desire to secure better buy-in, improve collaboration or strive for consensus, then emphasis on the political dimensions of the project initiation process may be most appropriate and meaningful.

Where there is an intent to enhance objectivity and improve the discipline and rigour by which individual project opportunities are evaluated, then an emphasis on the process dimensions may be more relevant. And where there is a need to pursue the evaluation and assessment of projects that are risky, that are politically sensitive, that represent significant change or that require strong levels of advocacy and commitment in order to proceed, then improving the influence of the project shaper role may be most appropriate. The value the organization seeks will provide guidance as to the approach and solution that will be most meaningful.

Implications of Improving Project Initiation Decisions

In conducting the research that led to the findings presented in this book, I uncovered significant variations in how projects are initiated and the influences on how initiation decisions are made. The process of project initiation is a fascinating one that inhabits a middle ground between the development of organizational strategy and the management of individual projects. Project initiation decisions are shaped by organizational forces of process and politics, but these decisions are also strongly influenced by the personal actions and influences of those who champion and support opportunities as they evolve from idea to initiated project. Whilst I speculated at the start of the research that there would be some personal influences on the initiation process, I did not expect to see the magnitude of personal impact that in fact emerged. The role of project shaper was present in every organization, to varying degrees, and had strong influences in its own right, as well as serving to augment organizational capabilities. The findings that result have strong implications, both for those who assume the project shaper role and for the executives who initiate ideas and ultimately decide whether or not to proceed with projects.

IMPLICATIONS FOR PROJECT SHAPERS

In the context of this study, the most significant findings – and by far the greatest challenges – existed for project shapers. Very few participants in the study indicated that the process of project initiation within their organization was very effective. The vast majority of organizations described by participants had project initiation processes that could be best described as 'not effective'. The study offers a number of areas of guidance for those who are involved in the project shaper role:

- **Presence of the role** – Perhaps the most important insight to emerge from this study is that there actually is a role called 'project shaper'. Every participant acknowledged the role as existing to some degree, although in some organizations it was viewed as being relatively informal. It was also a role that was variously played by sponsors, project managers and subject matter experts. The objective of the project shaper is to guide the project and provide support and encouragement through the project initiation process. It is a role that combines aspects of champion, steward and advocate, supporting the project while ensuring that the project meets the stated objectives of the organization. By recognizing the role, we begin to provide people with the insight, support and guidance necessary to perform it effectively.

- **Informality of the role** – The role of project shaper tended to be most informal in organizations that did not have a well-formed and effective rule system to support the process of project initiation. Not only did the small amount of process that was in place provide minimal guidance, there was often little recognition or consistency in how project initiation occurred. The political environment often created its own challenges, resulting in the initiation of any given project requiring even more effort, and likely facing even greater significant levels of scrutiny. When the role is informal it is more difficult to perform, as there is less support and a greater level of political uncertainty.

- **The intertwined roles of politics and proces**s – One of the important insights of the study is the degree to which politics and process are intertwined. The majority of participants indicated that politics had a strong influence on the project initiation process. Many participants indicated some level of process governing the approach to project initiation, although in many instances these were early, formative and inconsistently adhered to. Processes of varying degrees of formality were identified even where the rule emphasis within the organization was implicit rather than explicit. This indicates that the project shaper needs to clearly distinguish between whether an implicit or explicit rule system is in place, and the degree to which the political environment is constructive rather than antagonistic. One of the critical tasks for project shapers is to recognize the political environment within the organization, and align their approach accordingly.

- **The role of agency in project initiation** – A significant finding of this study regards the role of agency in supporting the process of project initiation. Agency, or the perceived flexibility with which participants believed they are able to act, was what enabled individual actors to work within, around or outside the rule environment of the organization in order to support the project initiation process successfully. Participants were able to contribute to enhancing the effectiveness of the rule system depending upon the process environment, influence of politics and rule system emphasis within the organization. The role of agency can at times support the system in place, and in other contexts may compensate for inadequacies of process or challenges of politics.

- **The opposing influence of high levels of formality and consistency** – While the study has identified the significant role agency can play in influencing the project initiation process, it also shows that agency has the potential to work counterproductively. In organizations with very formal and very consistent initiation processes, the rule system was in effect defined by the process environment. The high levels of rigour and expectations of adherence also suggest that the organization would not look favourably upon those who worked around or at cross-purposes to the process. In this context, participants indicated that much less flexibility was available, and described much more circumscribed instances where agency was constrained. In the face of difficult politics and little recognition of the formal role, assuming high levels of agency may represent a high-risk proposition. In other words, while agency can compensate for inadequate process and inappropriate politics, there are also scenarios where the use of agency is inappropriate.

IMPLICATIONS FOR EXECUTIVES

For executives, the insights of the study emphasize the development and reinforcement of the rule environment within the organization. As observed above, rule systems – whether implicit or explicit – operate at varying levels of effectiveness within organizations. The study offers considerations for executives from several key perspectives:

- **Role in establishing and maintaining the rule system** – Executives, through explicit direction or implicit behaviour, create and shape the rule systems in their organizations. As the study has demonstrated, many of the challenges in projects have to do with the clarity of the overall initiation process, how decisions are made within that process, and the degree to which the project shaper role is formally recognized. While implicit processes may be perceived as desirable in order to maintain flexibility and responsiveness, providing clarity about the process and its expectations – and the criteria for initiation decisions – can help those who shape projects to provide better and more effective input into the process. Work in the initiation process can focus on what is necessary to answer relevant questions at an appropriate level of detail, without repetitive rework and deferrals. At the same time, clarity of expectations means that participants in the process can better recognize when some projects should not proceed, eliminating the need to waste time trying to justify projects that are conceptual non-starters. In all instances, these changes will result in greater clarity, efficiency and transparency of the decision making process itself.

- **Participation in the political environment** – The study has clearly illustrated the role politics plays in the project initiation process. While politics was a dominant feature in the majority of participant descriptions, of particular significance was the number of examples of obstructive political environments, particularly in terms of avoidance and disagreement. Paying attention to the political environment, and endeavouring to provide constructive and positive discussion about points of contention, would have had a significant impact on the ability of many study participants to perform their roles effectively.

- **Managing conflicting messages in partially implemented rule systems** – In many participant organizations, the process of project initiation was relatively new or still being implemented. For these organizations, there was often a level of conflict perceived between legacy implications and new process expectations. Consciously attending to changes in expectations, particularly in the change from one rule regime to another, would create a much more transparent environment. While change management challenges cannot be avoided, they can be ameliorated.

Conclusions

The overall implications of this study are numerous, and have significant implications for those organizations seeking to improve how they make project initiation decisions. In particular, there is no single right answer to how best to evaluate and decide on whether to proceed with projects. Process factors, political factors and the agency of the project shaper have all been demonstrated to influence initiation decisions. Strong process, with high levels of process formality and consistency, can result in effective initiations, but this comes at the cost of constraining the autonomy, influence and flexibility – the agency – of those in the project shaper role. Constructive politics can influence initiation decisions, but the decision results are often characterized as being only somewhat effective, although the effectiveness of initiation decisions can be augmented by the personal agency of whoever is charged with the role of shaping the project and championing its development. Strong agency on its own was demonstrated in several instances to lead to effective initiation decisions, but this placed a great deal of responsibility on the shoulders of the individual serving as project shaper. Rather than relying upon organizational qualities, the emphasis was on personal abilities and influence. As a result, the quality and effectiveness of the decision making process was a direct result of individual effort, and was comparatively more difficult to replicate and support on a broad basis in organizations.

Ultimately, the process of supporting and making project initiation decisions needs to be appropriate for the individual organization. There needs to be an understanding of the organization's culture and environment, and consideration of the values that are most important in deciding to proceed with a project. What works will ultimately be the approach that is most directly aligned with the culture of the organization and what is most directly cared about in evaluating project opportunities.

Influencing the evolution of how project initiation decisions are made is also a significant challenge. Because of the strategic importance and significance of determining what projects to undertake, any shift to this approach will represent a significant organizational change that requires the investment of considerable political capital to bring about. There will be champions of this change, and there will be opponents. For the change to be successful, there needs to be sufficient support by a critical mass of the organizational executive. On a personal level, everyone involved in the process needs to recognize that they must also change their behaviours. This will require letting go of current levels of influence, autonomy and power in making initiation decisions and getting projects started, in favour of a more organizational approach. For many, this will be a shift into the unknown, requiring different approaches and practices. There will be different influences on the initiation process, and the process itself will lead to different outcomes as it responds to different priorities.

If organizations are to improve the effectiveness of their project initiation decisions, the people who make the decisions and hold the balance of power within those organizations must be supportive of the change. They must choose to change how projects are initiated, because by doing so, the organization – and by extension, themselves – will be better off. There needs to be an appreciation of the problems that need to be addressed – whether in terms of capacity, priority, value or relevance – and a belief that the new approach will address these problems effectively. Above all, there needs to be a willingness to make personal changes, collaborative changes and process changes, in the belief that doing so will make the organization more effective and will lead to more appropriate and relevant decisions. Doing so requires a careful consideration of those influences – of process, of politics, and above all of personal agency – that have the greatest impact on making effective initiation decisions. It is my hope that this book will provide the context to understand these influences, their implications and their interactions, and supply appropriate guidance to undertaking this important – if challenging – journey.

Bibliography

Andersen, E.S., Dysvik, A. & Vaagaasar, A.L. (2009). 'Organizational Rationality and Project Management'. *International Journal of Managing Projects in Business*, 2(4), 479–92.

Artto, K. & Wikström, K. (2005). 'What is Project Business?' *International Journal of Project Management*, 23(5), 343–53.

Artto, K., Kujala, J., Dietrich, P. & Martinsuo, M. (2008). 'What is Project Strategy?' *International Journal of Project Management*, 26(1), 4–11.

Artto, K., Kulvik, I., Poskela, J. & Turkulainen, V. (2011). The Integrative Role of the Project Management Office in the Front End of Innovation'. *International Journal of Project Management*, 29(4), 408–21.

Aubry, M., Sicotte, H., Drouin, N., Vidot-Delerue, H. & Besner, C. (2012). 'Organisational Project Management as a Function within the Organisation'. *International Journal of Managing Projects in Business*, 5(2), 180–94.

Barnard, C.I. (1938). *The Functions of the Executive* (30th anniversary edn). Cambridge, MA: Harvard University Press.

Bourgeois, L.J.I. & Eisenhardt, K.M. (1988). 'Strategic Decision Processes in High Velocity Environments'. *Management Science*, 34(7), 816–35.

British Psychological Society (2009). *Psychological Testing Centre Test Report: Insights Discovery Preferences Evaluator*.

Brunsson, N. (1982). 'The Irrationality of Action and Action Rationality: Decisions, Ideologies and Organizational Actions'. *Journal of Management Studies*, 19(1), 29–44.

Burns, T.R. & Dietz, T. (1992). 'Cultural Evolution: Social Rule Systems, Selection and Human Agency'. *International Sociology*, 7(3), 259–83.

Cicmil, S. (2006). 'Understanding Project Management Practice through Interpretative and Critical Research Perspectives'. *Project Management Journal, 37*(2), 27–37.

Cicmil, S. & Hodgson, D. (2006). 'New Possibilities for Project Management Theory: A Critical Engagement'. *Project Management Journal, 37*(3), 111.

Cicmil, S., Hodgson, D., Lindgren, M. & Packendorff, J. (2009). 'Project Management behind the Facade'. *Ephemera: Theory & Politics in Organization, 9*(2), 78–92.

Cohen, B.H. (2008). *Explaining Psychological Statistics* (3rd edn). Hoboken, NJ: John Wiley & Sons.

Cohen, M.D., Burkhart, R., Dosi, G., Egidi, M., Marengo, L., Warglien, M. & Winter, S. (1996). 'Routines and Other Recurring Action Patterns of Organizations: Contemporary Research Issues'. *Industrial & Corporate Change, 5*(3), 653–88.

Cohen, M.D., March, J.G. & Olsen, J.P. (1972). 'A Garbage Can Model of Organizational Choice'. *Administrative Science Quarterly, 17*(1), 1–25.

Cooper, R.G., Edgett, S.J. & Kleinschmidt, E.J. (2000). 'New Problems, New Solutions: Making Portfolio Management More Effective'. *Research Technology Management, 43*(2), 18–33.

Corbin, J. & Strauss, A. (2008). *Basics of Qualitative Research* (3rd edn). Thousand Oaks, CA: Sage Publications.

Crawford, L., Hobbs, B. & Turner, J.R. (2006a). 'Aligning Capability with Strategy: Categorizing Projects to Do the Right Projects and to Do Them Right'. *Project Management Journal, 37*(2), 38–50.

Crawford, L., Morris, P., Thomas, J. & Winter, M. (2006b). 'Practitioner Development: From Trained Technicians to Reflective Practitioners'. *International Journal of Project Management, 24*(8), 722–33.

Creswell, J.W. (1998). *Qualitative Inquiry and Research Design: Choosing Among Five Traditions*. London: Sage Publications.

Cyert, R.M. & March, J.G. (1992). *A Behavioral Theory of the Firm* (2nd edn). Malden, MA: Blackwell Publishing (first published 1963).

Cyert, R.M., Simon, H.A. & Trow, D.B. (1956). 'Observation of a Business Decision'. *Journal of Business, 29*(4), 237–48.

Dietz, T. & Burns, T.R. (1992). 'Human Agency and the Evolutionary Dynamics of Culture'. *Acta Sociologica, 35*(3), 187–200.

Eisenhardt, K.M. (1989a). 'Agency Theory: An Assessment and Review'. *Academy of Management Review, 14*(1), 57–74.

Eisenhardt, K.M. (1989b). 'Making Fast Strategic Decisions in High-velocity Environments'. *Academy of Management Journal, 32*(3), 543–76.

Eisenhardt, K.M. & Bourgeois, L.J.I. (1988). 'Politics of Strategic Decision Making in High-velocity Environments'. *Academy of Management Journal, 31*(4), 737–70.

Fayol, H. (1949). *General and Industrial Management.* London: Pitman (first published 1916).

Flyvbjerg, B. (2008). 'Curbing Optimism Bias and Strategic Misrepresentation in Planning: Reference Class Forecasting in Practice'. *European Planning Studies, 16*(1), 3–21.

Flyvbjerg, B. (2009). 'Survival of the Unfittest: Why the Worst Infrastructure Gets Built – and What We Can Do about It'. *Oxford Review of Economic Policy, 25*(3), 344–67.

Flyvbjerg, B., Bruzelius, N. & Rothengatter, W. (2003). *Megaprojects and Risk: An Anatomy of Ambition.* Cambridge: Cambridge University Press.

Flyvbjerg, B., Garbuio, M. & Lovallo, D. (2009). 'Delusion and Deception in Large Infrastructure Projects: Two Models for Explaining and Preventing Executive Disaster'. *California Management Review, 51*(2), 170–93.

Fredrickson, J.W. (1984). 'The Comprehensiveness of Strategic Decision Processes: Extension, Observations, Future Directions'. *Academy of Management Journal, 27*(3), 445–66.

Fredrickson, J.W. (1986). 'The Strategic Decision Process and Organizational Structure'. *Academy of Management Review, 11*(2), 280–97.

Fredrickson, J.W. & Mitchell, T.R. (1984). 'Strategic Decision Processes: Comprehensiveness and Performance in an Industry with an Unstable Environment'. *Academy of Management Journal, 27*(2), 399–423.

Gavetti, G., Levinthal, D. & Ocasio, W. (2007). 'Neo-Carnegie: The Carnegie School's Past, Present, and Reconstructing for the Future. *Organization Science, 18*(3), 523–36.

Heugens, P.P.M.A.R. & Lander, M.W. (2009). 'Structure! Agency! (And Other Quarrels): A Meta-analysis of Institutional Theories of Organization'. *Academy of Management Journal, 52*(1), 61–85.

Jung, C.G. (1971). *Collected Works of C.G. Jung, Volume 6: Psychological Types*. Princeton, NJ: Princeton University Press.

Kahneman, D. (2003). 'A Psychological Perspective on Economics'. *American Economic Review, 93*(2), 162–8.

Kahneman, D. (2011). *Thinking, Fast and Slow*. Toronto: Doubleday Canada.

Kahneman, D. & Tversky, A. (1979). 'Prospect Theory: An Analysis of Decision under Risk'. *Econometrica, 47*(2), 263–91.

Langley, A., Mintzberg, H., Pitcher, P., Posada, E. & Saint-Macary, J. (1995). 'Opening Up Decision Making: The View from the Black Stool'. *Organization Science, 6*(3), 260–79.

Lehtonen, P. & Martinsuo, M. (2008). 'Change Program Initiation: Defining and Managing the Program–organization Boundary'. *International Journal of Project Management, 26*(1), 21–9.

Lindgren, M. & Packendorff, J. (2009). 'Project Leadership Revisited: Towards Distributed Leadership Perspectives in Research'. *International Journal of Project Organisation and Management, 1*(3), 285–308.

March, J.G. (1987). 'Ambiguity and Accounting: The Elusive Link between Information and Decision Making'. *Accounting, Organizations & Society, 12*(2), 153–68.

March, J.G. & Simon, H. (1993). *Organizations* (2nd edn). Cambridge, MA: Blackwell Publishers (first published 1958).

Martynov, A. (2009). 'Agents or Stewards? Linking Managerial Behavior and Moral Development'. *Journal of Business Ethics*, 90(2), 239–49.

Maylor, H. (2001). 'Beyond the Gantt Chart: Project Management Moving On'. *European Management Journal*, 19(1), 92–100.

McCray, G.E., Purvis, R.L. & McCray, C.G. (2002). 'Project Management under Uncertainty: The Impact of Heuristics and Biases'. *Project Management Journal*, 33(1), 49–57.

Miller, D. & Sardais, C. (2011). 'Angel Agents: Agency Theory Reconsidered'. *Academy of Management Perspectives*, 25(2), 6–13.

Milosevic, D.Z. & Srivannaboon, S. (2006). 'A Theoretical Framework for Aligning Project Management with Business Strategy'. *Project Management Journal*, 37(3), 98–110.

Mintzberg, H., Raisinghani, D. & Théorêt, A. (1976). 'The Structure of "Unstructured" Decision Processes'. *Administrative Science Quarterly*, 21(2), 246–75.

Morris, P.W., Jamieson, A. & Shepherd, M.M. (2006). 'Research Updating the APM Body of Knowledge 4th Edition'. *International Journal of Project Management*, 24(6), 461–73.

Morris, P.W.G. (1989). 'Initiating Major Projects: The Unperceived Role of Project Management'. *International Journal of Project Management*, 7(3), 180–85.

Muller, R., Spang, K. & Ozcan, S. (2009). 'Cultural Differences in Decision Making in Project Teams'. *International Journal of Managing Projects in Business*, 2(1), 70–93.

Nelson, R.R. & Winter, S.G. (1973). 'Toward an Evolutionary Theory of Economic Capabilities'. *American Economic Review*, 63(2), 440–49.

Nelson, R.R. & Winter, S.G. (1974). 'Neoclassical vs. Evolutionary Theories of Economic Growth: Critique and Prospectus'. *Economic Journal*, 84(336), 886–905.

Nelson, R.R. & Winter, S.G. (2002). 'Evolutionary Theorizing in Economics'. *Journal of Economic Perspectives, 16*(2), 23–42.

Nutt, P.C. (1993a). 'Flexible Decision Styles and the Choices of Top Executives'. *Journal of Management Studies, 30*(5), 695–721.

Nutt, P.C. (1993b). 'The Formulation Processes and Tactics used in Organizational Decision Making'. *Organization Science, 4*(2), 226–51.

Packendorff, J. (1995). 'Inquiring into the Temporary Organization: New Directions for Project Management Research'. *Scandinavian Journal of Management, 11*(4), 319–33.

Pitsis, T.S., Clegg, S.R., Marosszeky, M. & Rura-Polley, T. (2003). 'Constructing the Olympic Dream: A Future Perfect Strategy of Project Management'. *Organization Science, 14*(5), 574–90.

Ross, J. & Staw, B.M. (1993). 'Organizational Escalation and Exit: Lessons from the Shoreham Nuclear Power Plant'. *Academy of Management Journal, 36*(4), 701–32.

Shenhar, A.J. (2001). 'One Size Does Not Fit All Projects: Exploring Classical Contingency Domains'. *Management Science, 47*(3), 394.

Simon, H.A. (1955). 'A Behavioral Model of Rational Choice'. *Quarterly Journal of Economics, 69*(1), 99–118.

Simon, H.A. (1959). 'Theories of Decision-making in Economics and Behavioral Science'. *American Economic Review, 49*(3), 253–83.

Simon, H.A. (1965). 'Administrative Decision Making'. *Public Administration Review, 25*(1), 31–7.

Simon, H.A. (1987). 'Two Heads are Better Than One: The Collaboration between AI and OR'. *Interfaces, 17*(4), 8–15.

Simon, H.A. (1997). *Administrative Behavior: A Study of Decision Making Processes in Administrative Organizations* (4th edn). New York: The Free Press (first published 1947).

Smith, C. & Winter, M. (2010). 'The Craft of Project Shaping'. *International Journal of Managing Projects in Business, 3*(1), 46–60.

Söderlund, J. (2004). 'Building Theories of Project Management: Past Research, Questions for the Future'. *International Journal of Project Management, 22*(3), 183–91.

Starbuck, W.H. (1983). 'Organizations as Action Generators'. *American Sociological Review, 48*(1), 91–102.

Steffens, W., Martinsuo, M. & Artto, K. (2007). 'Change Decisions in Product Development Projects'. *International Journal of Project Management, 25*(7), 702–13.

Thomas, J. (1998). 'It's Time to Make Sense of Project Management'. In *Proceedings of the Third Biannual Conference of the International Research Network on Organizing by Projects (IRNOP III), Calgary, Alberta*. Umeå, Sweden: IRNOP.

Thomas, J. & Mengel, T. (2008). 'Preparing Project Managers to Deal with Complexity: Advanced Project Management Education'. *International Journal of Project Management, 26*(3), 304–15.

Thomas, J. & Tjäder, J. (2000). 'On Learning and Control: Competing Paradigms or Co-existing Requirements for Managing Projects in Ambiguous Situations?' In *Proceedings of the Fourth Biannual Conference of the International Research Network on Organizing by Projects (IRNOP IV), Sydney, Australia*. Umeå, Sweden: IRNOP.

Thomas, J., Delisle, C.L., Jugdev, K. & Buckle, P. (2002). 'Selling Project Management to Senior Executives: The Case for Avoiding Crisis Sales'. *Project Management Journal, 33*(2), 19–28.

van Marrewijk, A., Clegg, S.R., Pitsis, T.S. & Veenswijk, M. (2008). 'Managing Public–private Megaprojects: Paradoxes, Complexity, and Project Design'. *International Journal of Project Management, 26*(6), 591–600.

von Neumann, J. & Morgenstern, O. (1944). *Theory of Games and Economic Behaviour* (60th anniversary edn). Princeton, NJ: Princeton University Press.

Vuori, E., Artto, K. & Sallinen, L. (2012). 'Investment Project as an Internal Corporate Venture'. *International Journal of Project Management, 30*(6), 652–62.

Walker, D.H.T., Anbari, F.T., Bredillet, C., Söderlund, J., Cicmil, S. & Thomas, J. (2008a). 'Collaborative Academic/practitioner Research in Project Management: Examples and Applications'. *International Journal of Managing Projects in Business*, 1(2), 168–92.

Walker, D.H.T., Cicmil, S., Thomas, J., Anbari, F. & Bredillet, C. (2008b). 'Collaborative Academic/practitioner Research in Project Management: Theory and Models'. *International Journal of Managing Projects in Business*, 1(1), 17–32.

Weick, K.E. (1995). *Foundations for Organizational Science: Sensemaking in Organizations*. Thousand Oaks, CA: Sage Publications.

Williams, T.M., Klakegg, O.J., Magnussen, O.M. & Glasspool, H. (2010). 'An Investigation of Governance Frameworks for Public Projects in Norway and the UK'. *International Journal of Project Management*, 28(1), 40–50.

Winter, M., Andersen, E.S., Elvin, R. & Levene, R. (2006a). 'Focusing on Business Projects as an Area for Future Research: An Exploratory Discussion of Four Different Perspectives'. *International Journal of Project Management*, 24(8), 699–709.

Winter, M., Smith, C., Morris, P. & Cicmil, S. (2006b). 'Directions for Future Research in Project Management: The Main Findings of a UK Government-funded Research Network'. *International Journal of Project Management*, 24(8), 638–49.

Winter, S.G. (1971). 'Satisficing, Selection and the Innovating Remnant'. *Quarterly Journal of Economics*, 85(2), 237–61.

Index

Page numbers in **bold** refer to figures. Numbers in parentheses in the case study section refer to case numbers listed on page 42.

For Product Safety Concerns and Information please contact our EU
representative GPSR@taylorandfrancis.com Taylor & Francis Verlag GmbH,
Kaufingerstraße 24, 80331 München, Germany

Printed and bound by CPI Group (UK) Ltd, Croydon, CR0 4YY

01/05/2025
01858391-0003